Petra Deimer

Parrots

Everything about Purchase, Acclimation,
Nutrition, and Diseases

With 28 Color Photographs by Outstanding Animal
Photographers and 30 Drawings by Fritz W. Köhler

Translated by Robert and Rita Kimber

Woodbury, New York/London/Toronto/Sydney

First English language edition published in 1983 by Barron's Educational Series, Inc.
© 1979 by Gräfe and Unzer GmbH, Munich, West Germany

The title of the German book is *Papageien*.

All inquiries should be addressed to:
Barron's Educational Series, Inc.
113 Crossways Park Drive
Woodbury, New York 11797

Library of Congress Catalog Card No. 83-14966
International Standard Book No. 0-8120-2630-6

Library of Congress Cataloging in Publication Data

Deimer, Petra.
   Parrots: everything about purchase, acclimation, nutrition, and diseases.

   Translation of: Papageien.
   Includes index.
   1. Parrots. I. Wolter, Annette. II. Title.
SF473.P3D5313   1983   636.6′865   83-14966
ISBN 0-8120-2630-6

Cover photo: Scarlet Macaw and Caninde Macaw
Inside front cover: African Grey Parrot
Inside back cover: A lovebird in flight
Back cover: Above, left: Greater Sulphur-crested Cockatoo; above, right: Blue-fronted Amazon. Below, left: Caninde Macaw; below, right: The author with her African Grey Parrot

Cover design: Constanze Reithmayr-Frank

Photographs
Angermayer: Back cover (above, right)
Bechtel: Page 28 (above, left)
Chaffer: Page 64 (above, right)
Coleman/Burton: Back cover (below, left)
Coleman/Reinhard: Inside back cover
Deimer: Page 28 (below, right)
Dossenbach: Pages 63, 64 (above, left)
de Grahl: Pages 9, 46
Lauert: Page 28 (above, right), back cover (below, right)
N.H.P.A./Blossom: Inside front cover
N.H.P.A./Baglin: Page 64 (below, right)
N.H.P.A./Morcombe: Page 64 (below, left)
Reinhard: Back cover (above, left)
Schmidecker: Front cover, pages 10 (above, right and below, left), 27
Schrempp: Page 10 (above, left and below, right)
Dr. Strunden: Page 28 (below, left)
Wothe: Page 45

PRINTED IN JAPAN

345   230   98765432

Contents

Preface

The subject of this handbook for pet owners is an exotic bird that many people would like to have but that is not the easiest creature to keep. This book deals specifically with those species of large and small parrots that are somewhat less difficult to keep and that can be bought in pet stores everywhere.

Parrots are frequently kept as pets, and it is not unusual for individuals to have more than one parrot. Keeping parrots, however, is a demanding business that requires a great deal of time and patience, and it is not everyone who has sufficient amounts of either. The owner of a budgerigar or canary deals with a domestic bird that has been bred in captivity for generations. The owner of some parrots, however, may have to cope with a wild bird that was probably flitting about in the jungles of its native habitat only a few months ago. He has on his hands a bird that has not yet digested the drastic change from a native biotope in the African, Australian, or South American jungles to a cage in a living room, a bird that will therefore tend to be very shy because its past experience with human beings has been bad. The author of this book describes in detail how much patience and effort she had to invest with her parrot Vasco before she could win his confidence and make him hand tame.

Parrots are "intelligent" and cannot be treated like birds on a lower level of biological development, nor can they be trained like a dog and taught to obey. If they make a nuisance of themselves in the home—chewing on valuable furniture, for example, or nipping holes in clothing or biting through electrical wires—this is usually because they are bored. Only if your parrot is properly occupied will he refrain from doing things that can damage your home or be harmful to him. Ornithologists agree that the parrot disorder known as "feather plucking" in which the bird plucks out all its own feathers is psychic in origin. Any parrot owner who does not keep this in mind, who leaves his bird sitting in its cage all the time, and talks to it only rarely through the bars will inevitably wind up with a phlegmatic pet that will become both physically and mentally ill within a short time. Also, the bird will give him very little enjoyment because it will learn only a few words or may not learn to talk at all.

This book takes in all the popular varieties of parrots, such as cockatoos, macaws, and Amazons, as well as the small varieties like the lories and lovebirds. Because of their different origins, these birds differ in their natures and in their nutritional needs. It is also crucial that the parrot owner understand the behavior of his feathered pet, and the special chapter "Understanding Parrots" provides the key to comprehending these amusing, exotic, and appealing birds.

How Parrots Come to Us

In their native countries, parrots have been kept as domestic birds since time immemorial. In the jungle villages of the Amazon basin, for example, almost every Indian hut has its pet parrot. Indian women take parrot chicks from their nests and raise them on *chicha*, an Indian beer made from boiled sweet potatoes.

The indiscriminate capturing of parrots by animal dealers and native peoples and the changes in, and destruction of, their habitat have brought some varieties of parrots to the verge of extinction. Dealers will stoop to any method of capturing the birds as long as it is quick and effective. They cut down trees to rob nests and burn a sulfur smudge until the birds fall out of the trees unconscious and can be picked up off the ground like dropped apples. About a million parrots are caught every year for sale as pets. Up to 50% of these birds die as a result of capture and shipment. Among young birds, the mortality rate is even higher. Concern about this high mortality rate is causing an improvement in shipping and housing conditions.

Customs, Quarantine, Banding

Every imported parrot has to be examined by the U.S. Department of Agriculture. With commercially imported birds, this routine examination is done following a 30-day quarantine period. After quarantine every parrot is given a numbered band that certifies that the bird has been legally imported and has in fact been examined by a USDA veterinarian as required by law. Any imported parrot without a band should be regarded as a potentially contraband bird that may have been illegally imported. The most important reason for examining birds after import is to see if they have Newcastle Virus, which is a threat to the U.S. poultry industry.

Spare your parrot the discomfort of wearing his band. Remove it as soon as you have your bird at home. He will eventually bite through the band anyway, and he can injure himself with it. It is quite sufficient if you keep the band available among your other documents.

The band is an annoyance for your parrot. Take it off before your bird bites through it or injures himself on it.

How Parrots Come to Us

The "Red List"

Human beings have already destroyed many kinds of animals, and others have been decimated to the point where only token numbers remain. Human greed has reduced some parrot species to extinction, and others are found only rarely. These remaining rare varieties have been placed on the international "Red List" of animals threatened with extinction. The Convention on International Trade in Endangered Species of Wild Fauna and Flora, drawn up in Washington, D.C., in 1973, forbids trade in the endangered species named in the convention. The following parrot species are included:

Kakapo, *Strigops habroptilus*
Thick-Billed Parrot, *Rhynchopsitta pachyrhyncha*
Cuban Amazon, *Amazona leucocephala*
St. Vincent Amazon, *Amazona guildingii*
Puerto Rican Amazon, *Amazona vittata*
Dominican Amazon, *Amazona arausiaca*
Yellow-shouldered Amazon, *Amazona barbadensis*
Imperial Amazon, *Amazona imperialis*
Red-browed Amazon, *Amazona dufresniana rhodocorytha*
Pretre's Amazon, *Amazona pretrei*
Vinaceous Amazon, *Amazona vinacea*
Red-tailed Amazon, *Amazona brasiliensis*
Blue-throated Conure, *Pyrrhura cruentata*
Lear's Macaw, *Anodorhynchus leari*
Glaucous Macaw, *Anodorhynchus glaucus*

Pileated Parrot, *Pionopsitta pileata*
Queen of Bavaria, *Aratinga guarouba*
Mauritius Parakeet, *Psittacula krameri echo*
Golden-shouldered Parrot, *Psephotus chrysopterygius*
Orange-bellied Parrot, *Neophema chrysogaster*
Maroon-fronted Parrot, *Rhynchopsitta terrisi*
Double Eyed Fig Parrot, *Opopsitta diophthalma coxeni*
Red-fronted Parakeet, *Cyanoramphus novaezelandiae*
Yellow-fronted Parakeet, *Cyanoramphus auriceps forbesi*
Night Parrot, *Geopsittacus occidentalis*
Fernando Po Grey Parrot, *Psittacus erithacus princeps*
Caninde Macaw, *Ara glaucogularis*
Red-fronted Macaw, *Ara rubrogenys*
Yellow-eared Conure, *Ognorhynchus icterotis*

As of June 6, 1981, all other species could be entered into trade only if supplied with export documents from the exporting countries. These species are listed in Appendix II of the Convention. At the third convention conference, which was held in New Delhi in March 1981, the following three species were excepted from these regulations:

Budgerigar, *Melopsittacus undulatus*
Cockatiel, *Nymphicus hollandicus*
Indian Ringneck Parakeet, *Psittacula krameri*

Descriptions of the Most Popular Parrot Species

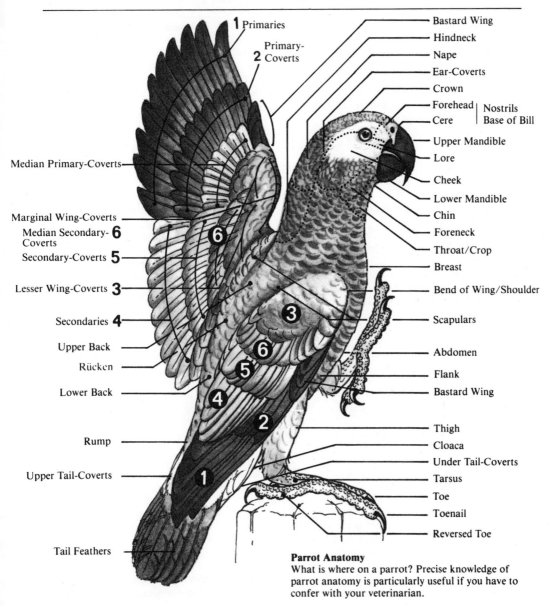

1 Primaries
Primary-
2 Coverts

Median Primary-Coverts

Marginal Wing-Coverts
Median Secondary- 6
Coverts
Secondary-Coverts 5

Lesser Wing-Coverts 3

Secondaries 4

Upper Back
Rücken

Lower Back

Rump

Upper Tail-Coverts

Tail Feathers

Bastard Wing
Hindneck
Nape
Ear-Coverts
Crown
Forehead | Nostrils
Cere | Base of Bill
Upper Mandible
Lore
Cheek
Lower Mandible
Chin
Foreneck
Throat/Crop
Breast
Bend of Wing/Shoulder
Scapulars
Abdomen
Flank
Bastard Wing
Thigh
Cloaca
Under Tail-Coverts
Tarsus
Toe
Toenail
Reversed Toe

Parrot Anatomy
What is where on a parrot? Precise knowledge of
parrot anatomy is particularly useful if you have to
confer with your veterinarian.

It is not easy, even for someone familiar with parrots, to find one's way through the labyrinth of families, genera, and species into which the various kinds of parrots are classified. The zoological schema given here, based on the classification used by K. Kolar in Grzimek's *Animal Life (Tierleben)*, is offered in hopes of providing the reader with a kind of road map to parrot classification.

Class: Birds, Aves
Order: Parrots and Allies, Psittaciformes
Family: Parrots, Psittacidae
Subfamily: Kea and Kaka, Nestorinae
Subfamily: Vulturine Parrot or Bristlehead, Psittrichasinae
Subfamily: Cockatoos, Cacatuinae
Subfamily: Pygmy Parrots, Micropsittinae
Subfamily: Lories and Lorikeets, Trichoglossinae
Subfamily: Owl Parrot or Kakapo, Strigopinae
Subfamily: All other Parrots, Psittacinae

The largest subfamily, Psittacinae, is further subdivided into the following tribes:
Tribe: Rosellas and Allies, Platycercini
Tribe: Wax-billed Parrots, Loriini
Tribe: Bat Parrotlets or Hanging Parakeets, Loriculini
Tribe: Blunt-tailed Parrots, Psittacini
Tribe: Wedge-tailed Parrots, Araini

The seven subfamilies comprise 75 genera, 326 species, and 816 subspecies.
  Many parrot species are already extinct, and many others are exported from their native countries only rarely, if at all, because they are on the "Red List." In the following descriptions, I have included only those parrots that make good house pets and that are easily obtainable in pet stores. The body length given always refers to the overall measurement from the beak to the tip of the tail.

Cockatoos (Subfamily Cacatuinae)

Popular genera:

Palm Cockatoo (*Probosciger aterrimus*), Length: 32 in (80 cm)
Black Cockatoos (*Calyptorhynchus*), Length: 20–26 in (50–65 cm)
  Popular subspecies: Yellow-tailed Black Cockatoo (*Calyptorhynchus funereus funereus*); White-tailed Black Cockatoo (*C. f. baudinii*)

White Cockatoos (*Cacatua*)
  Popular species: Greater Sulphur-crested Cockatoo (*Cacatua galerita*), Length: 20 in (50 cm); Lesser Sulphur-crested Cockatoo (*C. sulphurea*), Length: 14 in (35 cm); Salmon-crested Cockatoo (*C. moluccensis*), Length: 20 in (50 cm); Rose Breasted Cockatoo or Galah (*C. roseicapilla*), Length: 15 in (38 cm); Little Corella (*C. sanguinea*), Length: 16 in (40 cm); Umbrella Cockatoo (*C. alba*), Length: 16–18 in (40–45 cm); Leadbeater's Cockatoo (*C. leadbeateri*), Length: 15 in (38 cm)

Gang-Gang Cockatoo (*Callocephalon fimbriatum*), Length: 14 in (35 cm)
Cockatiel (*Nymphicus hollandicus*), Length: 12 in (30 cm)
  There is debate among ornithologists on whether the Cockatiel should be classified among the cockatoos or not.

Geographical origin: Cockatoos are native to Australia, New Guinea and its neighboring islands, eastern Indonesia, the Moluccas, and the Philippines. Depending on their genus and species, cockatoos live on timbered mountain slopes, in rain forests, or in open forests. In some areas, cockatoos have become a plague to farmers because they are seed-eaters and will often destroy entire fields.
Special characteristics: The name cockatoo derives from a Malayan word meaning "pliers" or "vise"

and referring to the bird's powerful beak. Cockatoos nest in large, deep holes high up in hollow trees. In most parrot species only the female incubates the eggs, but male and female cockatoos share this chore. The Palm Cockatoo is not only the largest of the cockatoos but also has the longest beak (4 in or 10 cm) of all the parrots. The cockatoo's most striking feature is its erectile crest, which it raises when excited or frightened. The beak of the cockatoo differs from that of other parrots in that the lower mandible is wider than the upper.

Suitability as a pet: Cockatoos are very popular but also very demanding pets. They are gregarious birds, and if they are kept singly they will readily develop attachments to humans. But if they do not get the company they need, they will be unhappy and pine away. They are usually not exclusive with their favors and will enjoy contact with a number of people. They want to be petted often and a lot, enjoy gestures of affection, and like to keep busy. They are very affectionate and playful and can put on amusing acrobatic shows. Because they are agile climbers, they need a tree to tumble about on; and being powerful fliers they need sufficient space to fly in. Some very tame cockatoos have been kept in complete freedom in their owners' yards. Their excellent sense of direction, their attachment to people they know, and constant vocal contact with familiar people keep them from flying away. Cockatoos can also be kept in a large outdoor aviary equipped with a room where they can get warm and be out of the weather. If a cockatoo in an aviary will not have much contact with people, it cannot be kept alone. Cages, aviaries, and nesting boxes have to be made of extremely durable materials because the cockatoo's powerful beak can chew through the hardest objects. It is possible to breed cockatoos, but breeding pairs become so pugnacious that even familiar people are not safe from attack.

Talent for speech: The literature on parrots is in general agreement that cockatoos are not as gifted for speech as Amazons or Grey Parrots. Of the cockatoos, the Little Corella is reputed to be the most able talker. Some varieties of cockatoos can shriek quite loudly. Also, they will imitate all kinds of sounds and can learn to whistle.

Life expectancy: Over fifty years.

Preferred foods: Sunflower seeds, wheat, oats, millet, canary seed, lettuce, dandelion greens, chickweed, carrots, fruit (especially cherries), willow twigs, and other twigs to gnaw on.

Lories and Related Birds
(Subfamily Trichoglossinae)

Popular genera:

Fig Parrots (*Psittaculirostris*), Length: 6–8 in (16–20 cm)
Fig Parrots (*Oppopsitta*)
    Popular species: Double-eyed Fig Parrot (*Oppopsitta diophthalma*), Length: 5½ in (14 cm)

Lorikeets (*Chalcopsitta*), Length: 12–13 in (30–32 cm)
Lorikeets (*Eos*), Length: 10–12 in (25–30 cm)
Lorikeets (*Trichoglossus*), Length: 7½–11 in (19–28 cm)
    Popular species: Swainson's Blue Mountain Lory (*Trichoglossus haematodus moluccanus*), Length: 13 in (32 cm); Red-collared Lorikeet (*T. h. rubritorquis*), Length: 13 in (32 cm); Ornate Lory (*T. ornatus*), Length: 9 in (23 cm)

Lories (*Domicella*), Length: 11–12 in (28–30 cm)
    Popular species: Black-capped Lory (*Domicella lory*), Length: 12 in (30 cm); Chattering Lory (*D. garrula*), Length: 12½ in (31 cm)

Lorikeets (*Charmosyna*), Length: 6–16 in (15–40 cm)

Geographical origin: Southeastern Australia, New Guinea and neighboring islands.

Special characteristics: The lories are among the most colorful of parrots. Some varieties have brilliant coloration; others, however, are unobtrusive,

Descriptions of the Most Popular Parrot Species

and some are black. Depending on the species, body length can range from 5 to 16 inches (12 to 40 cm). Lories differ from other parrots in having not a thick, muscular tongue, but one tipped with papillae that is better adapted to the nectar, pollen, and soft fruits that are their major sources of food. The upper mandible has no "filing notches" (see **page 56**) or only minimal ones. Lories, of which there are sixty-one known species and 160 subspecies, are sociable birds, and even in the wild they are not particularly shy. Most species are skillful fliers and good climbers.

Suitability as a pet: Many bird lovers keep lories in their aviaries primarily because these birds are so beautiful. They are friendly and lose their shyness of human beings, but they cannot be relied upon to accept people as companions. The difficulties of keeping lories in our living quarters works against close ties between them and their owners. Lories produce large amounts of mushy and sometimes watery droppings. This makes it hard to keep their surroundings clean, and the hygienic problems they create make it inadvisable to keep a single lory in a house or apartment. Lories should, instead, be kept in pairs in a spacious outdoor aviary that must, however, include a frost-proof refuge. Lories cannot be kept together with birds of other species or even with other types of lories. Most lories, but particularly the Blue Mountain Lory (*Trichoglossus haematodus moluccanus*), lead lively and playful lives in an aviary. They also enjoy long and frequent baths. Sturdy nesting boxes can also serve as sleeping quarters. There have been some few successful attempts to breed Blue Mountain Lories in Europe.

Talent for speech: If Black-capped Lories and Chattering Lories have a lot of contact with their keeper, they will become attached to him and will also learn to speak. Other lory species are not noted for their speaking ability, and a shrill whistle is the sound natural to them.

Preferred foods: Softened zwieback or egg bread enriched with honey and vitamins. Fruit pressed through a strainer (baby food); sweet fruit; berries; grated, cooked carrots; dried ant pupae; cooked rice; biscuit. Supplements of slightly sprouted sunflower seeds, sprouted oats, and some canary seed can be gradually introduced into the strained fruit. Lories like to eat on the ground, and their food should be offered to them at beak height above the ground.

Rosellas and Allies (Platycercini)
(Tribe of the subfamily Psittacinae)

Popular genera:

Budgerigar (*Melopsittacus undulatus*), Length: 7–8 in (18–20 cm)
Grass Parrots (*Neophema*), Length: 8–9 in (21–22 cm)
   Popular species: Turquoise Parrot (*Neophema pulchella*); Elegant Parrot (*N. elegans*); Bourke's Parrot (*N. bourkii*)
New Zealand Parrots (*Cyanoramphus*), Length: 9–12 in (23–30 cm)
Psephotus, Length: 9–12 in (24–30 cm)
Red-capped Parrot (*Purpureicephalus spurius*), Length: 13–14 in (32–36 cm)
Rosellas (*Platycercus*), Length: 13–14 in (32–36 cm)
   Popular species: Eastern Rosella (*Platycercus eximius*); Crimson Rosella (*P. elegans*); Port Lincoln Parrot (*P. zonarius*)

Geographical origin: Depending on genus and species, the rosellas and related birds inhabit widely divergent regions of Australia, and some of them occur in New Zealand.

Special characteristics: All the Platycercini are richly colored birds that show a wide variety of colorations and markings. In 1960, the Australian government sought to protect these splendid creatures by prohibiting their export. Still, some species continue to reach the European market illegally. Some Platycercini species and genera can be bred in captivity. An example is the budgerigar, on which I will not go into further detail here because there are other books devoted entirely to this bird. The reader with zoological interests may, however, be

Descriptions of the Most Popular Parrot Species

surprised to discover that this most popular of all pet birds belongs to the class of true parrots. Almost all Platycercini are skillful and powerful fliers, but they are not as good climbers as the larger parrots. Grass Parrots are ground birds that live in the thick underbrush of the forest. Birds of the genus *Cyanoramphus* are ground dwellers, too, and are quick and agile on their feet.

Suitability as a pet: Species of the genus *Psephotus*, Rosellas, and the Red-capped Parrot can be kept only in a spacious outdoor aviary that includes a warm room. These birds have a strong need to fly that cannot be met indoors, much less in a cage. Grass Parrots and the *Cyanoramphus* genus, too, should be kept in an outdoor aviary; as ground dwellers they require a lot of space to run in. There are probably more Turquoise Parrots living in aviaries today than there are in the wild. Because of their quiet temperament, they can be kept indoors if they are acclimatized to indoor living as chicks. But they still require adequate flying time every day.

Talent for speech: Some species can learn to speak a few words, but none of these birds can be called real talkers. Rosellas have a very pleasant voice, however, and the *Psephotus* genus is noted for its song.

Preferred foods: Depending on the species, these birds like grass seed, canary seed, millet, and oats, also sprouts made from all of these. The larger species also like sunflower seeds and small or crushed nuts. Other foods that can also be offered are zwieback, lettuce, parsley, dandelion greens, chickweed, berries, fruit, and carrots. Willow twigs (and twigs from other trees) should be provided for gnawing.

Parakeets (Psittacula)
(Genus of the subfamily Psittacinae; Tribe: Wax-billed Parrots, Loriini)

Most popular species: Alexandrine Parakeet (*Psittacula eupatria*), Length: 18 in (45 cm); Plum-headed Parakeet (*P. cyanocephala*), Length: 14 in (35 cm)

Geographical origin: Moist, forested regions of India, southeastern Asia, and Africa. Some species live in high mountain ranges; others can be found in villages.

Special characteristics: Birds of this genus are typical tree dwellers and, as such, are good fliers and climbers. They nest in hollow trees. After hatching their eggs, they live in large flocks. The sexes cannot be distinguished from each other until the birds are about two years old and changes in plumage make sex identification possible. The male Alexandrine Parakeet has a colored neck ring that is lacking in the female. The male Plum-headed Parakeet has a bluish green neck band; the female, a yellowish one. These parakeets were imported into Europe and sold at high prices even in antiquity.

Suitability as a pet: If young birds of this genus are kept singly they become very tame. However, they require a lot of attention, activity, outdoor flying, and a tree to climb in. Because of the strong need for flight and climbing, pairs are best kept in a spacious outdoor aviary. If they are gradually accustomed to cold, they can tolerate quite low temperatures; but if the thermometer drops to around freezing, the birds have to have a warm indoor area available to them. They have been bred in captivity. Caution! These parakeets do not get on well with other varieties of parrots, and any birds that are smaller than they will be in real danger in their company. The Plum-headed Parakeet is the only one of these parakeets capable of peaceful coexistence.

Talent for speech: These parakeets can learn to speak very well. The males are reputed to be better talkers than the females. The sounds they produce naturally are pleasant flute-like notes and a kind of twittering.

Preferred foods: Mixed seeds, such as sunflower seeds, oats, wheat, millet, canary, and hemp; fruit, lettuce, herbs, chickweed, dandelion greens, zwieback, biscuit, small or crushed nuts, green twigs for gnawing.

Descriptions of the Most Popular Parrot Species

Lovebirds (*Agapornis*)
(Genus of the subfamily Psittacinae;
Tribe: Wax-billed Parrots, Loriini)

Popular species: Black-winged Lovebird
(*Agapornis taranta*), Length: 6 in (16 cm); Red-
faced Lovebird (*A. pullaria*), Length: 5½ in
(14 cm); Peach-faced Lovebird (*A. roseicollis*),
Length: 6½ in (17 cm); Grey-headed Lovebird
(*A. cana*), Length: 5½ in (14 cm); Masked
Lovebird (*A. personata*), Length: 6 in (15–16
cm); Fischer's Lovebird (*A. fischeri*), Length:
6 in (15–16 cm); Nyasa Lovebird (*A. lilianae*),
Length: 6 in (15–16 cm); Black-cheeked Lovebird
(*A. nigrigenis*), Length: 6 in (15–16 cm)

Geographical origin: Africa and Madagascar. Some
species live in forests; others, in the desert; still
others, in the mountains.
Special characteristics: The name tells it all: These
little parrots maintain an unusually close bond with
their sexual partners. When lovebirds are not
nesting, pairs of them will live in small groups of
from ten to forty birds. They nest in hollow trees,
termite dens, or nests abandoned by other birds.
All lovebirds are a brilliant green; the differences
that mark the various species are evident in the
plumage of the head and sometimes of the throat.
Some species stand out because of the white ring
around the eye. Sexual differences are difficult to
detect. Lovebirds are skillful fliers, climbers, and
runners.
Suitability as a pet: Some authors claim that a
single lovebird that is raised from its earliest days
with humans will become very tame and friendly. If
this is to happen, though, the bird has to be in
almost constant contact with the human that serves
as a substitute for its mate. Other authors say it is
cruelty to animals to keep lovebirds singly. Pairs,
too, can easily adjust to human society, but they
need ample space and opportunity to climb and fly.
Watching these amusing birds that tend each other
and play together incessantly is a thoroughly enjoyable pastime. Lovebirds fare very well in a
spacious outdoor aviary, but the aviary has to include space that is tight against wind and rain and
that can be heated to at least 60°F (15°C) in the
winter. Some species have been bred successfully,
even to the point of introducing color variations.
Some caution is in order if lovebirds are to be kept
in a communal aviary. If they are put together with
other lovebird species or other kinds of birds, they
can become aggressive and may even start biting off
their aviary-mates' toes.
Talent for speech: Ranges from mediocre to none
at all. However, lovebirds have a very pleasant
voice that sometimes expresses itself in a delightful
chirping.
Preferred foods: Sunflower seeds, canary seed,
millet (prepared food for small parrots), hulled and
whole oats (also sprouted), lettuce, parsley,
chickweed, dandelion greens, sweet fruits, carrots,
and green twigs for gnawing.

Eclectus Parrots (*Lorius*)
(Genus of the subfamily Psittacinae,
Tribe: Wax-billed Parrots, Loriini)

Most popular species: Grand Eclectus Parrot
(*Lorius roratus*), Length: 16 in (40 cm)

Geographical origin: Dense jungles in northern
Australia, New Guinea, and in neighboring archi-
pelagoes.
Special characteristics: The males have green
plumage, the females, red. These parrots are loners
and pair up only at nesting time. They are good
fliers and climbers and breed very high in hollow
trees.
Suitability as a pet: Eclectus Parrots should only be
kept singly. In human company, they become tame
and trusting. Even older birds will adapt easily.
Eclectus Parrots in captivity do not fly much, but
they do climb a lot, making a climbing tree an absolute necessity. Newly imported birds are very sensitive to cold and should be kept at room

Descriptions of the Most Popular Parrot Species

temperature (68–72 °F [20–22 °C]). If they are frightened and in poor condition as a result of capture and shipping, they require very careful attention. Once they have adapted to their new environment, they can tolerate lower temperatures but never freezing or below. Eclectus Parrots will flourish in an outdoor aviary only in the summer months, but even in this season the aviary has to have a heated shelter where the bird can go at night and during cold and rainy periods.

Talent for speech: Eclectus Parrots can learn to talk. Their natural voice is pleasant and not piercing.

Preferred foods: The mainstay of the diet is fruit, such as grapes, rose hips, currants, and berries from the mountain ash, also carrots, raw or cooked corn, lettuce, chickweed, dandelion greens, and parsley. In captivity, an Eclectus will learn to accept seeds, too (especially sprouted sunflower seeds), but will then require a lot of drinking water as well.

Senegal Parrot (*Poicephalus senegalus*),
Length: 9½ in (24 cm)
(Genus of the subfamily Psittacinae, Tribe: Blunt-tailed Parrots, Psittacini)

Genus: Long-winged Parrots, *Poicephalus*

Geographical origin: Southern West Africa.
Special characteristics: Senegal Parrots are gregarious birds and live in flocks. The sexes have somewhat different plumage, and the males have a somewhat larger bill.

The wings, breast, and back of the Senegal Parrot are bright green; the belly and under tail-coverts, yellow; the cheeks, light gray; the head, dark gray. The bill is gray with a black point. Senegal Parrots are popular pets and are imported in large quantities.

Suitability as a pet: Young birds will become exceptionally tame and will, even in flight, follow their owners around. Only birds that are older when imported will remain shy and unruly. If they are kept as single birds, Senegal Parrots need a lot of human contact, play, and activity. They also need a climbing tree and natural branches on which they can gnaw every day. During the acclimatization period, they are sensitive to cold and have to be kept at room temperature (68–72 °F [20–22 °C]). Pairs or a group of birds can be kept year round in an outdoor aviary. In the winter, however, they need a heated interior room and constant protection from wind and dampness. Senegal Parrots have been bred in captivity but not with such great success that no further imports are necessary.

Talent for speech: Senegal Parrots are not particularly gifted mimics, but they can learn some words and imitate sounds. Their natural voice is powerful but not disturbing.

Life expectancy: Ten to fourteen years.

Preferred foods: Sunflower seeds, millet, canary seed, peanuts, also mixed prepared foods for large parakeets, fruit of all kinds, lettuce, dandelion greens, chickweed, and—for gnawing—willow, lilac, elder, birch, and fruit-tree twigs.

Amazons (*Amazona*)
(Genus of the subfamily Psittacinae, Tribe: Blunt-tailed Parrots, Psittacini)

Popular species: Blue-fronted Amazon (*Amazona aestiva*), Length: 14–16 in (35–41 cm); Yellow-fronted Amazon (*A. ochrocephala*), Length: 14 in (35 cm); St. Lucia Amazon (*A. versicolor*), Length: 14–15 in (35–38 cm); Red-lored Amazon (*A. autumnalis*), Length: 14 in (35 cm); Yellow-shouldered Amazon (*A. barbadensis*), Length: 13½ in (34 cm); Vinaceous Amazon (*A. vinacea*), Length: 14 in (35 cm)

Geographical origin: Central and South America and some neighboring islands. According to species, Amazons live in dense jungles or open

Descriptions of the Most Popular Parrot Species

forests. They prefer river valleys in moderate to hot climates.

Special characteristics: Amazons live in "extended families," but pairs remain together within the group. At nesting time, the pairs withdraw from the group and seek out their usual nesting place. Amazons are clumsy runners and fliers, but they are are excellent climbers. A black or dark brown iris is a sign of a young bird. In adults, the iris is yellowish. Depending on species, the bright green plumage is varied with red, yellow, white, or blue patches on the head, cheeks, and throat or on the shoulder and under tail-coverts. It can, however, take several years before the plumage of the adult bird reaches its full coloration.

Suitability as a pet: Together with the African Grey, the Amazons are the most popular parrots for pets. Many of them that have been raised by humans in the country of their origin are already tame by the time they are imported. Others will still be shy and frightened. But once they are tame, they make likeable and affectionate house pets. If they are kept in a relatively small area, they tend to give up flying almost altogether; but care should still be taken, for I know of a few cases in which Amazons have escaped and flown away. They are excellent climbers, and a climbing tree with strong branches is an absolute necessity. On the ground, Amazons waddle about comically and turn somersaults. Because they breed in caves and hollows, they like to find a cave-like corner in the apartment where they can hide. Amazons need a lot of activity and human attention or another bird as a companion. This companion can, for example, be an African Grey, provided there is no antipathy between the individuals. Newly imported Amazons have to be kept at room temperature (68–72 °F [20–22 °C]). The temperature can later be lowered to 60 °F (15 °C). Amazons have been bred in captivity, and even crossbreeding has been successful. Anyone who wants to breed Amazons will have to keep a small group of them at room temperature in a spacious indoor aviary. If a pair show a willingness to breed, they have to be separated from the rest of the group and provided with the conditions necessary for brooding, the essential ones being quiet and constant warmth.

Talent for speech: Opinion about the speaking ability of Amazons is widely divided. There is credible evidence that Amazons, like the African Grey, can learn to speak and even to use their vocabularies logically and appropriately. In his book *King Solomon's Ring*, Konrad Lorenz tells of his experiences with a verbally gifted Amazon. As with all parrots that are able to speak, this ability can vary immensely from one Amazon parrot to another. The bird emits its shrill natural cry most often when he is bored. If frightened, the Amazon produces a distinctive shriek.

Life expectancy: Over fifty years.

Preferred foods: Sunflower seeds, oats, wheat (also sprouted), canary seed, small amounts of hemp seed, millet, peanuts, walnuts, and hazel nuts. Sweet fruits of any kind, radishes, carrots, kohlrabi, tomatoes, fresh peas in the pod, lettuce, parsley, chickweed. For gnawing, willow, elder, lilac, poplar, and fruit-tree twigs.

African Grey Parrot (*Psittacus erithacus*), Length: 14 in (36 cm)
(Genus of the subfamily Psittacinae, Tribe: Blunt-tailed Parrots, Psittacini)

Geographical origin: Forested areas of equatorial Africa.

Special characteristics: Grey Parrots are gregarious birds that live in pairs and in flocks and forage for food together. They live in trees, breeding in hollows they find there. They are good fliers but do not have much endurance. They are excellent climbers. Although they are not brilliantly colored birds—their red tail feathers provide the only touch of color in their basically gray plumage—they are among the most popular species and are famous for their speaking ability.

Suitability as a pet: The younger an African Grey is

Descriptions of the Most Popular Parrot Species

when it comes into contact with humans, the more unconditionally it will accept a human as its "partner." Very young birds can be recognized by their black or gray irises. Older birds have a yellowish or orange-colored iris. Grey Parrots kept singly need close contact with their primary partner but will be friendly with other members of the family as well. A single bird has to be included within the family's sphere of activity. African Grey Parrots that spend their lives confined to a cage or chained to a perch may be bored and waste away or tear out their own feathers. Along with human affection, they need a lot of activity, wood to gnaw on, appropriate toys, a climbing tree, adequate exercise, and a roomy cage from which they are released every day.

Two Greys can become tame and friendly; however, they can be very choosy about their partners. Sometimes they will develop an undying antipathy toward one of their own kind, and you cannot rely on just any two birds getting along as partners or as a pair. If the African Grey is to learn to talk, he should be kept alone. The pleasure he takes in speech will not dwindle, however, if he is given a partner later on. It is difficult to tell the sexes apart. Even when exceedingly tame, the African Grey remains somewhat untrusting. With his excellent memory, he nurses grudges, and he may not forget mistreatment for years afterward. Keeping Greys in an aviary makes sense only if two or more birds can live together and maintain contact with each other. It will happen only rarely that a pair will form and breed because African Greys will pair only for "true love."

Talent for speech: No other species surpasses the African Grey in speaking ability, the Amazons being the only other parrots that begin to rival the Grey. One must always keep in mind, however, that speaking ability always remains an individualized talent that will be more or less developed in different birds. Tame Greys imitate all kinds of sounds: the barking of dogs, the songs of wild birds, the ringing of a telephone, doors creaking, people coughing. They can whistle complete tunes, imitate the voices of the people they know, and ap-

ply their vocabularies in a logical and appropriate way. A properly cared-for African Grey will not often emit its loud, natural cry, but it will betray its moods with a soft croaking sound or, sometimes, with growling tones.

Life expectancy: Fifty to seventy years.

Preferred foods: Sunflower seeds, prepared mixes for large parrots, whole peanuts, halved walnuts in the shell, carrots, corn, kohlrabi, radishes, tomatoes, lettuce, parsley, chickweed, fruit, especially kiwis, bananas, grapes, cherries, tangerines, and apples. Dried biscuit, zwieback, occasional meat leftovers on cooked bones, a little lean chicken, a little hard cheese. An essential source of vitamins is the bark of twigs from lindens, willows, pines, lilacs, and fruit trees.

Parrotlets *(Forpus)*
(Genus of the subfamily Psittacinae, Tribe: Wedge-tailed Parrots, Araini)

Popular species: Green-rumped Parrotlet (*Forpus passerinus*); Length: 5 in (13 cm); Mexican Parrotlet (*F. cyanopygius*), Length: 5 in (13 cm); Pacific Parrotlet (*F. coelestis*), Length: 4½ in (12 cm)

Geographical origin: Open woodlands of South America.

Special characteristics: The parrotlets of this genus are the next smallest of parrots after the pygmy parrots (Micropsittinae), which grow to a length of only four inches (10 cm). They live in small flocks and choose for nesting holes in the ground or abandoned ovenbird (*Furnarius rufus*) nests as well as hollow trees. Like other small parrots, they do not use their feet to hold things, such as their food. The sexes are easily distinguished because of their respective dull and brilliant plumage. This difference is evident even in young birds. The species listed above are yellowish green, light green, and dark green. The Mexican Parrotlet is yellowish green and has blue edges on its wings and dark blue

Descriptions of the Most Popular Parrot Species

secondaries. The Green-rumped Parrotlet is bright green and has blue under wing-coverts as well as blue secondaries. The Pacific Parrotlet is a light olive green, is light blue in the nape of the neck, and has light blue streaks at the temples. In all these birds, the wing tips cover the short wedge tail.

Suitability as a pet: Parrotlets caught in the wild and bred in captivity are both available in pet stores. The ones caught in the wild catch cold easily when subjected to the change in climate, and they are not as easy to tame as domestically bred parrotlets. Newly imported birds have to be kept at room temperature (68–72 °F [20–22 °C]) for at least a year. If you are concerned with acclimating your parrotlet to its new home, spend a lot of time with it each day, and keep it busy. This will result in an enjoyable and often touchingly affectionate companion. Well acclimated parrotlets can be kept in an outdoor aviary, but they need protection from wind and dampness and, in the winter, a heated indoor area. Parrotlets can be bred easily; however, the breed pair have to find each other highly compatible.

Talent for speech: A tame single bird that has a lot of human contact can learn to speak a few words, will imitate familiar sounds in a charming way, and has a soft natural voice.

Preferred foods: Prepared foods for small parrots (budgerigars), small sunflower seeds, hulled oats (also sprouted), carrots, sweet fruits, lettuce, dandelion greens, chickweed, parsley, softened figs, and various fresh twigs for gnawing.

Macaws (*Ara*)
(Genus of the subfamily Psittacinae, Tribe: Wedge-tailed Parrots, Araini)

Popular species: Chestnut-fronted Macaw (*Ara severa*), Length: 18–21½ in (45–52 cm); Scarlet Macaw (*A. macao*), Length: 31–35½ in (78–90 cm); Green-winged Macaw (*A. chloroptera*), Length: 31–35½ in (78–90 cm); Military Macaw (*A. militaris*), Length: 26 in (65 cm); Blue and Gold Macaw (*A. ararauna*), Length: 32½–37½ in (80–95 cm)

Best known species: Hyacinth Macaw (*Anodorhynchus hyacinthinus*), Length: 39 in (98 cm)

Geographical origin: Tropical areas and islands between Mexico and Brazil. Macaws are jungle dwellers that live in the neighborhood of river valleys.

Special characteristics: Macaws are the largest of all parrots; the Hyacinth Macaw, with its 39 inches, being the largest of the macaws. Macaws have a powerful bill that is in keeping with their large size. Also, in the true macaws (those of the genus *Ara*), the areas around the eye are not feathered but have a somewhat wrinkled skin. In some species this skin appears to have light markings on it. The Blue and Gold Macaw has striking, wavy black lines on this light skin. The Hyacinth Macaw has only narrow rings of skin around the eyes and the lower mandible. Macaws are gregarious, forage in large flocks, and sometimes inflict heavy damage on fruit and grain crops. Within the flock, pairs stay together for life. For nesting, they return to their large nesting caves that they use year after year. Aras are primarily climbers. They fly only when they are forced to or to cover large distances. With their waddling stride, they move about on the ground only with difficulty.

Suitability as a pet: Most macaws offered for sale are somewhat tame, having been caught as young

Descriptions of the Most Popular
Parrot Species

birds and raised by their captors in their home countries. Still, when we buy them, they have yet to get over the psychic strain of shipment, quarantine, and a new environment. With sympathetic treatment, though, they adapt quickly to their new homes, become friendly, and choose a particular friend from the people around them. The person a macaw chooses then has to devote considerable attention to the bird. Others should approach the bird with caution, because it will usually recognize only the selected person as its "substitute parrot." Macaws need a large cage with hardwood branches in it and a climbing tree made of hardwood branches as thick as your arm. Under no circumstances should you use a metal perch and chain.

A tame macaw will hardly ever leave a place he has adopted as his own, but he will climb about in it a great deal. At night, and if the bird has to be left alone for a few hours, he should be locked in his cage. Most macaws will hardly ever fly indoors, though they will flutter into the air if frightened. Macaws should get a lukewarm shower every day. An outdoor aviary is not any more appropriate for a single macaw than it is for a single parrot of any other species; the bird would pine away in it. Two or more macaws can live in an aviary, but they need a shelter for cool days and, in the winter, a spacious, heated room.

Talent for speech: A macaw that you raise by hand from youth will learn to speak, but it will usually be able to say only a few words, not entire sentences. The macaw's natural voice is loud and shrill, and even tame birds will let it be heard if they are frightened. The cries of shy, untamed macaws seem to cut to the very bone.

Life expectancy: Fifty to eighty years; some macaws have lived to be 100.

Preferred foods: Nuts, even ones with very hard shells, sunflower seeds, fresh corn on the cob or dried corn, wheat, oats. Sweet fruit of all kinds, carrots, kohlrabi, lettuce, chickweed, dandelion greens, zwieback, and, fresh every day if possible, willow, elder, beech, oak, and fruit-tree twigs for gnawing.

Considerations before You Buy

Are You Sure a Parrot Is for You?

There is no doubt that a pet, whether fish, flesh, or fowl, brings life into your house. But it is not always easy to meet the demands that a pet bird, mammal, or fish puts on its owner; and a pet must have the right to make demands of its owner because it did not, after all, choose to come live with you. You chose it. It needs its own living quarters, proper care, and a lot of attention. Delivering those things will cost you time, patience, and money.

If you find you do, in fact, want a parrot, you will surely prefer to have a lively, healthy, affectionate bird rather than one that does nothing but sit lethargically in its cage. Parrots are not easy to keep because, in most cases, they are not domestic creatures

but wild ones. Because wild birds and animals have not been bred by man for generations they are not adapted to life as domestic animals, and it takes a lot of tact and sensitivity to help them adjust to human beings and a man-made environment. Answer the following questions carefully. They will help you determine whether you have the makings of a good parrot owner.

Questions to Ask Yourself before You Buy

A parrot is the right pet for you only if you can answer all these questions with an honest and unqualified yes.

1. Are you fully aware that parrots are naturally gregarious, loyal, and intelligent birds that need either one of their own kind as a partner or, if they are kept alone, a substitute partner in the form of a human being, namely, you? If a parrot is left alone too much it will suffer from isolation and boredom. This can lead in turn to behavioral disorders and even to physical illness.

2. Do you have to be away at work for more than eight hours every day? If so, is some other member of your family at home all the time, or at least for a few hours, and is that person willing to spend some time with your parrot?

3. Do you have children or other family members who are qualified and willing to care for your parrot?

4. Does your landlord permit the keeping of domestic animals? Even if your parrot is always kept in your apartment, your neighbors will surely be aware of its presence because parrots can pro-

duce loud and penetrating shrieks. These are particularly likely in the first weeks that you have your bird.

5. Are you aware that some parrot species live as long as people and that your parrot might well outlive you? Did you know that they can often behave like small children that will never grow up and they respond to punishment with nothing but mistrust and fear?

6. Will you be able to provide first-class care for your parrot when you go away on vacation, if you have to go to the hospital for a while, or if you are prevented from coming home for some reason or another?

7. Are you the kind of person who likes to spend his free time at home and often does?

8. Do you have a healthy attitude toward dirt? Parrots generally cannot be housebroken (see page 58). They defecate wherever they happen to be. They shed feathers, particularly down, and they shake dust out of their feathers. They scatter bits of food and gnaw their twigs into chips. You will have to put up with all this without having fits or, worse yet, resolving to teach your bird some manners.

9: Will your parrot be more important to you than valuable furniture, intact wallpaper, paneled doors and ceilings, carpets, knicknacks, and curtains? All these things will be in danger from your bird's powerful bill and natural urge to be active, and they may well depreciate in value after their encounters with a parrot.

10. Will you still love your parrot even if it shows no interest in or talent for learning to speak?

Which Kind of Parrot Is the Right One for You?

After carefully questioning yourself, you find you do, in fact, want a parrot. Now you have to ask which kind of parrot is the right one for you and your household. Because parrots can differ greatly not only from species to species but also from individual to individual—that is, from one bird to another of the same species—the answer to this question can be only an approximate one at best.

Let's start with your house or apartment. I am sure you will agree that small animals are more appropriate to a small home, larger animals to a larger one. This holds true for parrots, too. Of the smaller birds, a cockatiel, two lovebirds, a parrotlet, or, of course, a budgerigar makes an excellent house pet.

For the giant of parrots, the macaw, you have to have a large apartment, for a macaw cage alone takes up a lot of space. And for any and every parrot you have to consider not only a place for its cage but also an area outside the cage where the bird can move about freely for at least four or five hours a day. In this area you should have a climbing tree constructed of strong, natural tree branches. Also, it is essential for your bird's physical conditioning that it have the opportunity to fly or walk about.

You should not get the impression from what I have just said here, however, that a tame parrot's space requirements are so immense that they can hardly be met at all. The

Considerations before You Buy

average living room is large enough for most species, provided that your parrot can share it with you, at least sometimes. Tame parrots will choose to spend most of their time in their familiar corner, which, in most cases, will be the climbing tree. They make only occasional sorties into the room, whether on foot or in the air.

Some parrots fly a lot; others prefer to walk or climb. Anyone who has a relatively small living area should not choose a bird whose preferred mode of locomotion is flying. The best choice in such circumstances is a bird that likes to climb. Birds of this type are of the short-tailed varieties that are usually referred to as "parrots" and differ from the long-tailed "parakeets" that enjoy flying and are good at it but that usually cannot climb very well. The smaller "parakeets" that are good fliers need sufficient space to move about in even in small rooms.

If you prefer a larger parrot that will not fly much indoors, you should choose an African Grey, an Amazon, a cockatoo, or, if you have enough room, a macaw. Remember, though, that with these varieties a climbing area is an absolute necessity.

I have mentioned only a few of the most common domestic parrots here. There are, of course, others you might consider, such as the parrotlets and the lovebirds, which should be kept only in pairs. If you will not be bothered by occasional flying expeditions the Alexandrine Parakeet, the Indian Ringnecked Parakeet, and the Plum-headed Parakeet make good house pets, too. Most of the other parakeets are best kept in groups in aviaries.

If you have a particular species in mind, then read the detailed description of this species in the preceding chapter.

What You Can Expect from a Parrot

Parrots differ in their suitability as pets. Some can be tamed more easily than others. But one principle is universally true: The younger a parrot is when it becomes accustomed to human company, the tamer it will become. Consequently, birds that are raised by a breeder will be best adapted to humans. Unfortunately, though, only a few species can be bred successfully. These are the lovebirds, parrotlets, cockatiels, and a few others. Most of the parrots available to us have been captured in the wild; and here, too, the young birds can be tamed much more easily than the older ones. Both the people who capture the birds and the pet dealers are fully aware of this, too; and most

Considerations before You Buy

of the birds for sale in pet stores are no longer shy of humans, having become partially tame either in their native country or in the pet store.

Every parrot owner wants a bird that will learn to talk, and almost every parrot species can learn to imitate syllables, words, sentences, or other sounds. Of primary importance in this "speech training" is that the bird trusts its owner and is tame. A frightened parrot will either be silent or will produce only its natural sounds. It will not imitate its master's voice. Do not begin with the assumption that you can go out and buy a "talker." There is no guarantee of speaking ability, and the literature is contradictory on this point. But if there is any bird that is most likely to become a good talker, it is the African Grey, although there are many Greys that have difficulty speaking or remain totally silent as the result of poor handling. And there are some Amazons and Indian Ringnecked Parakeets that have learned in the neighborhood of a hundred sounds. Many observers think that Greys have somewhat untrusting natures. It is certainly true that it takes more patience to win their confidence. The same is true of macaws. Amazons, Senegal Parrots, and cockatoos can be won over much more easily, and cockatoos have a reputation as the friendliest of all parrots. Other parrots that are easy to keep are the cockatiel and the Plum-headed Parakeet. But with all parrots, from the smallest to the largest, how they behave and how affectionate they are will depend largely—and this cannot be stressed enough—on how they are treated by human beings in general and by their owners in particular.

A Single Parrot or a Pair?

All parrots, large or small, are gregarious birds that cannot tolerate being alone. If no fellows of their own species are available, they will necessarily resort to substitute parrots, and this is the capacity in which you will function. If you will not be able to give a single bird a great deal of company, you should buy a pair right off. The disadvantage to this is that the birds will focus their attention on each other and will not develop as great an attachment to you as a single bird would. Also, two birds will not learn to speak as easily, unless one of them already knows how. A parrot that has formed a partnership with another member of its species in the pet store should not be separated from that partner. Both birds will pine, will not get over the loss of the partner for a long time, and will

Considerations before You Buy

therefore resist forming an attachment to a human. This is especially true of lovebirds, as their name suggests; and they should be kept only as pairs. If you want two parrots, buy them both at the same time. Buying another one later can be problematic if the two birds prove incompatible or develop a rivalry toward each other.

Advice for when You Buy

There is always an element of chance involved in buying a bird. Some experts claim that you should choose only those birds that have handsome plumage and make a reasonably lively impression. These signs often enable you to tell healthy from sick birds. And, of course, they should be kept in clean, spacious cages and aviaries. Other experts recommend buying a bird that not only gives the impression of health but that also takes in the world with calm attention and does not scream with fright when someone approaches its cage.

In my opinion, it is very likely that you can buy a parrot and find out only later that it has a cold or screams with fright. In either case, the proper handling—constant warmth, avoidance of drafts, chaos, and noise—will enable you to cure your bird's cold and win his confidence. I feel the most important thing is to get the youngest bird possible or one that is already accustomed to people. In some varieties, such as the Amazons, the plumage of very young birds will not yet have reached full color. In young Senegal Parrots and African Greys, the iris of the eye is still dark. It turns gray later, and in adult birds it is yellowish (see "Descriptions"). These older birds should be left to experienced hands who have been keeping parrots for a long time. Macaws offered for sale are almost always already tame. When you buy, ask your dealer what food the bird has been getting and take a few portions of it with you. Be sure that you buy a package of mixed food, too, regardless of what else the bird has been getting.

Your Parrot and Other Pets
How about a Dog?

If you want to have a dog, you should put off getting one until your parrot is fully accustomed to you and its surroundings. After a few disapproving glances, your parrot will accept, though probably never much like, the newcomer. The dog should be young so that he can be trained from the start not to chase the parrot. Once he has learned that and obeys your commands, he and the parrot may even become friends.

Considerations before You Buy

Inborn Fear of Cats

I would not advise keeping a cat and parrot together because you can never tell when the predator in the cat will come to the fore. Also, many parrots — with perhaps the exception of the large macaws — are afraid of cats because predatory cats are among their enemies in their native habitat. Consequently, even a tame parrot will be afraid at the sight of a cat. But despite all this, I know of households where a cockatiel and a cat curl up and sleep together, and the cat never even dreams of eating the bird. It should be noted, though, that such cats are lazy old lap cats that have long since given up catching mice, too.

Small Rodents

Small animals like rabbits, guinea pigs, and hamsters that do not number among the natural enemies of birds usually pose no problems. If your parrot should detest them, then you will have to keep the animals in another room, at least on those occasions when they have to be left alone. A rabbit or guinea pig clearly cannot do a large bird any harm, but a tame parrot may well show its dislike by slashing at the small, harmless animal.

Birds of a Feather and Other Feathers

It may or may not work out well if you acquire another parrot as company for your already established bird. Some parrot species get along well with other birds; some tolerate only their own species but attack others. Bringing birds together should be done with caution, and you should always be ready to intervene if necessary. Birds that are not familiar and friendly with each other should never be left together unsupervised for long periods of time.

Small varieties like parrotlets, cockatiels or budgerigars may approach a large bird in a curious and friendly way only to find that the larger bird will hack at them either in fear or to defend its territory. Some birds may be so totally imprinted to humans that they will not tolerate other birds.

What Your Parrot Needs for Its Well-Being

Your parrot cannot live in isolation from your family. If it is left alone, it will be lonely. You will have to get used to the idea that your living room is also a flying area. While some parrots kept in captivity may not fly as often or for such long stretches as they would in the wild, other species cannot do without their rapid circumnavigations. All parrots are more or less talented climbers, too. Some species often prefer to use their bills and legs more than their wings. But in any case a parrot has to have the opportunity both to climb and fly every day. First of all, though, it needs a cage that it can use as a base for exploring its new environment.

The Right Cage for a Parrot

Pet stores offer all kinds of parrot cages for sale, ranging from elaborately decorative cages to minuscule round cages to wooden, pagoda-like cages that a healthy parrot will destroy in no time at all.

Good parrot cages are expensive, and many dealers will be more intent on selling the customer something than on seeing he has the cage he really needs. If the price strikes the customer as too high, the dealer will often suggest a cheaper cage that is too small, assuring the customer all

A commercially available parrot cage. Dimensions: 16 x 16 x 30 inches (45 x 45 x 75 cm).

the time that the size has been proved adequate if not downright palatial. The fact of the matter is that large parakeets, African Greys, Amazons, cockatoos, and macaws need a cage that is at least 39 inches (100 cm) high and has a floor area at least 27 × 27 inches (68 × 68 cm). The height of the cage is more crucial than its depth. A cage measuring 16 × 24 × 39 inches (40 × 60 × 100 cm), for example, provides adequate climbing opportunities and could house two

Green-winged Macaw grooming its feathers. ▷

parrots. But if the cage is significantly smaller than this, it can be used for sleeping only.

There are innumerable poor models of these high, box-shaped cages, and tallying up all the things that are wrong with these models would fill pages. I will therefore try instead to tell you what you should look for in a cage rather than try to tell you what to avoid.

• The grating of the cage should be made of heavy steel wire. Ideally, it should be galvanized or chrome-plated. Grating covered with white plastic is not good because the parrot will gnaw the plastic off, and the unprotected metal under it will then rust.

• The cage roof should be flat so that your bird, once he is tame, can walk around on the roof. A domed roof offers no foothold. If you already have a cage with a domed roof, mount a branch on it for the bird to sit on. In pet stores and in the pet departments of department stores you can also buy perches that can be mounted on the cage roof.

• The cage should have more than one perch inside. Your parrot is no convict, and he should be able to enjoy himself inside his "castle." The perches should be placed so the bird can easily reach his food and water containers from them.

• If the cage contains a swing, leave it there at first. If your bird likes to use it, leave it. If he ignores it or if it bothers him, remove it.

• The cage should be equipped with two or three food and water containers. One container is for seeds, one for water, and one for fruit, greens, and other supplementary foods. You should be able to fill these containers from outside the cage because a bird that is not yet acclimated to his new home will be frightened if you reach into his quarters.

• The cage door is important. If it closes simply with a latch, your parrot will probably soon learn to open it himself. He will enjoy this immensely, particularly when he sees that the open door also leads to freedom. The door has to be equipped with a lock or snap that will keep it shut.

• The cage will usually have a grate installed above the floor. Experts disagree about the value of this arrangement. I feel it is not of much use, and I have removed it from my cage. Its only advantage is that the bird does not come in contact with his feces when he tries to pick at the sand on the floor underneath the grate. But then some feces inevitably get caught on the grate itself anyhow. The disadvantages are that birds with long tail

What Your Parrot Needs for Its Well-Being

feathers will ruin this plumage on the grate and that any bird will have difficulty reaching the limestone sand that is essential to his health. The sand has to be changed frequently anyhow. The worst of the feces have to be removed every day at the least and new sand scattered in the cage.

• A sturdy floor tray is practical in a parrot cage. The tray should be easy to remove for occasional thorough cleanings with hot water.

Just as important as a proper cage is its location in your apartment or house. The cage cannot be put on the floor because a parrot feels uneasy, if not actually endangered, if life goes on above his head. The cage should be at about eye level for someone standing up. Pet stores have metal tables or stands of the appropriate height that can be used as pedestals for cages, but be sure any stand you buy cannot be tipped over. If a stand meets this requirement, it may well be preferable to a small cabinet or table you already have on hand because your bird will be able to climb up and down on the metal framework of the stand.

Your new parrot will get used to his surroundings from the security of his cage. The cage door will remain shut at first, but it should not stay shut for too long. A parrot should not spend his life behind bars, but I do not mean to suggest either that your bird can dispense with his cage altogether later on. Having begun his life among humans in a cage, your bird will continue to regard his cage as his usual refuge, the place where he is fed and where he feels himself to be truly at home.

A Cover at Night?

The best place for a parrot to sleep is in his cage. Whether you put a cover over the cage at night is a question you should decide yourself. It is in the nature of these cave-nesting birds to want to be covered at night, and almost all parrots are. You should at least try covering your bird's cage at night. You will soon know whether he finds this annoying or not. I do not cover my African Grey, Vasco. Early attempts to do so evoked nothing but shrieks from him. He now sleeps without the cloth and not even inside his cage. He prefers to sleep in the open doorway of his cage. If he likes this uncomfortable arrangement, then he should have his way. That is our motto, and I am sure it is correct. Our Amazon, Manaos, on the other hand, insists on being covered for sleeping and will scream until we supply the cloth. When we first got Vasco, we tried all sorts of tricks to settle him in his cage at night; but after enough wild parrot

What Your Parrot Needs for Its Well-Being

chases around the living room, we gave up and let Vasco sleep the way he wanted to. We sometimes managed to catch him by using the upper part of his cage as a kind of butterfly net. But he soon caught onto this method and hid under a table where we, together with a large part of a cage, would not fit. By contrast, Manaos will let us take him out of his cage or put him back in. It is not a good idea to use force with a parrot or to be inconsiderate in outwitting him. Greys and macaws are particularly sensitive to mistreatment of this kind, and it quickly makes them suspicious of you.

The Proper Place for the Cage

Before your parrot moves into his cage, the cage has to find its proper permanent location. The cage should not be in the focal point of the family's activities but rather in a quiet corner that will provide your parrot with a good view of the room. Your bird will not keep to himself for long, though, for a tame parrot is eager for human companionship. The back of the cage should be placed against a wall, thus providing cover from the rear.

Parrots need bright daylight, and a place near a window is a good choice. But the cage must not be exposed to direct sunshine in the heat of the day. If the sunshine is streaming in through the window, the bird needs someplace where he can get into the shade. Otherwise he can suffer from the heat. For the same reason, the cage should not be too close to radiators or heating vents. A location too near a window is also harmful because flickering light and piercing noises can irritate your parrot. But the most important requirement of all for the location of the cage is that it not be in a draft. If there is no absolutely draft-free place in your living room, you will have to make it a strict household rule that the door not be left open and that only one window, preferably a screened one, can be opened.

The All-Important Climbing Tree

One thing that is essential for keeping a parrot is a climbing tree. Not only does it provide your bird with physical activity, but it will also evolve into a favored perch and lookout for him. You should choose for your climbing tree a gnarled branch that has a lot of twists and smaller branchings in it. The bark is an important part of the branch, for your bird will delight in peeling it off. The best branches come from fruit trees, willows, lindens, beeches, and maples. They make an important

What Your Parrot Needs for Its Well-Being

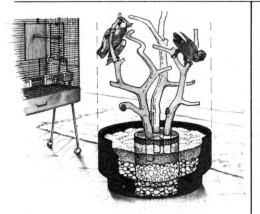

A large, homemade climbing tree for a parrot. For this design you need a tub filled with gravel and grit, a section of a log with holes bored in it, and three thick branches with the bark still on them.

contribution to your bird's nourishment as well as to his physical conditioning (see page 32).

As long as your bird continues to work on a branch, you can keep it; but once it has been gnawed clean, you should get a new one. Your parrot may be a little confused by the appearance of this new tree at first, but he will soon take to it, devising new climbing routes and finding new bark to remove. A bird that is kept busy with his tree will chew far fewer holes in your furniture. You can follow your own inclinations in devising a stand for the climbing tree. We use a tub filled with sand. This base is heavy enough to keep the whole structure from toppling over.

You can also use a Christmas tree stand or an umbrella stand. Or you can adopt the suggestion shown in the illustration on this page. New branches can simply be inserted into the holes in the log and wedged tight. One branch can reach over toward the cage and another toward the living room couch, for example. Your bird can then choose whether he will go back to his cage or take a walk on the furniture. Branches can also be attached directly to the cage.

Aviaries Indoors and Out

While an aviary is not to be recommended for a single parrot, it is quite ideal for a small flock of birds. Small parrots that like to fly and pairs of the larger species will find their needs well met by a spacious aviary. For the summer months, you can use a carefully caged-in balcony as a flying and climbing area. Or if you have a yard, you can build an aviary equipped with shelter against wind, rain, and cold nights and, for the winter, with a frost-free or heated room.

In an aviary, birds lead their own lives, limited though those lives may be, and therefore focus their attention more on each other than on their caretaker. Aviary parrots are not oriented to humans and are by no means as amusing as their fellows

What Your Parrot Needs for Its Well-Being

that have become members of human families. Still, parrot enthusiasts that have the space and have several birds should consider keeping pairs or groups in a spacious aviary. This is particularly desirable for the various species that go under the name of parakeets in pet stores.

An aviary provides birds with enough space to fly around in. This necessarily implies a quite large enclosure and not just a small one adequate for housing birds. How large the aviary has to be will depend on the kind and number of birds to be kept in it. Perches and climbing trees have to be on hand in an aviary, too, but they should not obstruct the flying area.

In addition to the outdoor aviary, parrots need an indoor aviary or shelter that can serve as a kind of bedroom or living room. The indoor and outdoor aviaries are connected by a doorway. A landing board or perch is placed in front of this "bedroom door" so that the birds can enter and leave their indoor room easily. This entryway should be located high up because parrots in the wild seek out high places to hide or sleep in. For this same reason, the warm shelter should be at a higher level than the outdoor aviary so that the birds will feel at ease in it. This shelter must keep out drafts,

A simple climbing tree that you can make yourself. The branch, pointed at the bottom, is stuck into a heavy Christmas-tree stand. The sleeping cage shown here is large enough for a single bird and is available in pet stores.

rain, excessive heat and cold, and, of course, be free of vermin. Daylight should reach the birds everywhere in the structure either through wire netting or large windows. Parrots do not thrive in darkness or dim light. Because they are used to a twelve-hour alternation of day and night in the wild, both the outdoor aviary and its attached shelter should be equipped with electric lights for the short winter days. Four o'clock in the morning has proved to be a good time for the automatic timer to turn the lights on. This prompts the parrots to begin their day early, and they then go to sleep with the normal sunset.

What Your Parrot Needs for
Its Well-Being

Most parrots cannot tolerate the temperatures of northern winters. Some species cannot be exposed to any frost, and others have to be kept at room temperature all year long. This means that the aviary shelter has to be equipped with heat if your parrots will be kept in the aviary year round.

The aviary should have a floor of concrete, PVC, or stone. This will prevent rats, mice, and other animals from burrowing into the aviary, for all kinds of rodents will be attracted by the birds' food.

Steel rods make the best framework for an outdoor aviary. The openings in the wire netting have to be quite small not only to prevent the birds from escaping but also to keep undesirable guests from entering. The parrot expert Wolfgang de Grahl recommends wire netting with intervals of 3/8" (9.5 mm) or hardware cloth with intervals of 1/2" (12.5 mm). The diameter of the wire should be at least 1/32" (0.7 mm) so that the birds cannot bite through it.

Introducing Birds into the Aviary

You will probably not start out by keeping a whole flock of birds in your aviary but will begin with a pair of one species. If you then introduce new birds into an aviary already occupied, you will have to be careful to see that the old and new birds are compatible both as species and as individuals (see page 34). New birds should never be introduced if the established pair is nesting because nesting birds are particularly inhospitable to newcomers.

This feeding dish made of plastic can be hung inside the cage.

Parrots will usually claim a certain area as their own, and it is a good idea to offer new birds an unoccupied area equipped with new branches. Initial clashes can also be avoided by clearing the aviary completely, rearranging it, and then putting the smaller, weaker birds back into it first. The stronger birds should be put in later. Another method is to keep new birds in a small cage for a while where they will be able to find their food and water easily. When they have made their initial adjustment, the entire cage, with the door open, can be put into the aviary. This provides the new birds with a refuge, and they can gradually explore the

What Your Parrot Needs for Its Well-Being

aviary and find their place in it using this refuge as a home base. Pairs of different species bother each other less than pairs of the same species, unless, of course, the birds of the same species naturally breed in colonies and always live in the company of their own kind. Many species get along well with neighbors when they are not brooding but avoid each other when they are raising their young.

"Underdogs" and bullies have to be removed from an aviary and housed elsewhere.

The Bird Room

If you have a spacious outdoor aviary with a frost-resistant shelter but cannot keep the shelter heated throughout the winter, you should consider equipping a room in your house as a bird room. You can then bring your entire parrot community inside during the winter. A room used for this purpose should be draft free and get enough fresh air and daylight.

The walls should be painted with a washable paint, and the window should have fine wire mesh on it so that you can air the room without letting any birds escape. Parrots are active during the day, and they need ample daylight hours in the winter, too. You therefore have to provide electric lighting to extend the daylight hours. And of course your bird room must be heated.

It is best if the floor has no cracks and can be easily cleaned. Window sills and doors of wood will not hold up to parrot bills for long. You will either have to replace them with a tougher substance or resign yourself to putting in new wood periodically. A bird room also needs all the amenities that you would normally provide in the shelter of your outdoor aviary. The ideal solution is an outdoor aviary connected to a bird room inside your house. Then your birds can go in and out as they please.

Taming Your Parrot and Adapting Him to His New Home

The Frightened Wild Bird

It is not easy to win the confidence of a bird that you have just purchased. Parrots are torn out of their natural habitat with rather crude methods, and their first impressions of human beings are far from favorable. Then they are exposed to more frightening experiences during shipment, in quarantine, and in the pet store. Not until your parrot is in your hands will he have encountered a human being who has his well-being at heart. It will require a great deal of affection and patience on your part to overcome the bird's mistrust. This process can take several months, a year, or possibly even longer.

The First Days at Home

Let me tell you about my experience with taming a shy parrot. Your first days and weeks with your new parrot may well be similar, though I hope they will not be quite so difficult. My African Grey, Vasco, proved to be a difficult case. If I had been faithfully following the advice of the experts I had read, I could not even have considered buying him. He sat apathetically in his cage, looking like a plucked chicken that had already experienced the worst and was expecting nothing better. But this was the parrot I wanted, and no other would do. Perhaps it was sheer pity that prompted me, a teenager inexperienced with parrots, to buy this utterly unpromising bird. The pet store owner agreed to take the bird back if my parents responded to my purchase with an irrevocable veto. I highly recommend this arrangement because there is nothing worse for a pet than being merely tolerated in its new home and not genuinely welcomed.

Now Vasco was sitting in his cage in our house. At first we could not come any closer to him than ten feet before he began screeching and flapping his wings wildly. He must have been in abject fear of us, and to our disappointment his fits of panic grew worse rather than better in his first few days with us. He had apparently abandoned his indifference to what might happen to him and was determined now to defend himself. The only thing you can do under these circumstances is leave your parrot in peace and express your affection for him from a distance. We tried to calm Vasco by speaking softly to him and avoiding rapid movements, loud noises, or anything else that could possibly reawaken his fears. Then one morning, after many days of extreme timidity on Vasco's part and extreme consideration on ours, our parrot produced a pathetic sounding mono-

Taming Your Parrot and Adapting Him to His New Home

tone whistle. This was the first sign that we had established some kind of contact with Vasco; and from then on we began to converse with him by whistling. He seemed to enjoy this acoustic exchange and began to whistle more and more often. We had done the right thing by not forcing ourselves on him and by letting him set the pace and tone in making friends.

After a few weeks we could come to within six feet of his cage without his falling into a panic, but the days when his cage had to be cleaned continued to be pure torture for him because we had to come much too close to him for his comfort.

Hand Taming Your Parrot

With time, any parrot that is well treated will lose his fear of his master or mistress, though I should add that there can be some rare exceptions to this rule. The bird learns that nothing unpleasant is going to happen when a human approaches him. This is the time when you can start getting him used to your hand. The best way to do this is to use the simple trick of offering him a treat through the bars of his cage, speaking softly as you hold out the morsel to him. Keep at this, even if your arm threatens to strike on you and go to sleep. You will have

to persist. I offered Vasco peanuts and fruit; and, of course, the trick did not work at first. Weeks had to pass before my problem child Vasco deigned to accept a nut from my hand. But then the spell was broken; his fear of my hand was gone, and at the same time he learned to tolerate my close presence.

The First Venture Outside the Cage

When your parrot has become hand tame — that is, when he will take food from your hand and is no longer frightened by your close proximity — then the time has come to open the cage door and let him enjoy the freedom of the living room. After all, you do not want him to be a stay-at-home that never leaves his cage.

But before you open the cage door for the first time be sure that your parrot's first flight does not end with a crash against an uncurtained window. Such an accident could, at the least, reawaken his old anxieties; and if he were flying fast enough, he could even injure himself seriously. So draw the curtains; or if there are no curtains, let the blinds down halfway, or put some object in front of the window to define the limits of the room.

Taming Your Parrot and Adapting Him to His New Home

The climbing tree will soon become your parrot's favorite perch. The tree also serves as a lookout and jungle gym and provides exercise for your bird's bill.

A bird that is not fully tamed will often be afraid when the cage door is first opened. Your parrot may be suspicious and not come out immediately. If he stays in his cage, offer him a treat the way you did to accustom him to your hand, this time, however, through the open door and not between the bars of the cage. By gradually drawing this bait out the door, you can lure your parrot out. He will soon be sitting in the open doorway. Curious now, he will start climbing around on the outside of the cage. He may even attempt a first flight right away. This will most likely end in a crash landing either because his wing feathers, clipped in the pet store, have not grown back enough yet or because, despite the flight exercise of flapping his wings in his cage, he has not used his wings in actual flight for a long time. If he lands on the rug, let him walk around there for a while. You might give him a nut or some seeds now to show him that this unknown territory can have its pleasant surprises, too. After a while, he will return to his cage himself. If he does not, put his cage down next to him on the floor so he can climb into it. You will be amazed at how quickly your parrot learns to enjoy the freedom of his new domestic biotope and to find his way home to his cage.

Perching on Your Hand or Arm

Once your parrot is used to leaving his cage, you can start putting your hand or arm in front of his feet. If you are patient and persistent, he will eventually climb up on it. He will quickly accept this new perch and will come readily to your arm or hand.

Taming Your Parrot and Adapting Him to His New Home

Vasco will climb only onto my arm. If I offer my hand, all he can think about is getting his head scratched, not perching.

When you have won your parrot over to the point that he enjoys leaving his cage, is not afraid of your hand, and will perch on your arm or shoulder, then the worst phase of his fear of humans has been left behind. From now on, you and your parrot will take increasing pleasure in your mutual friendship and will find more and more ways of cementing this new relationship between human and bird. It took a year for my problem parrot Vasco to become fully tame. He put

Large parrots are excellent climbers. If they want to reach their masters' shoulders, they often take the route via a trouser leg.

my patience to a very long test; but when I think of the many happy experiences I have had with him since then, I feel that my effort has been well rewarded. "He's tame," we all say now whenever Vasco begins at a visitor's toes and proceeds to climb up to his shoulders, whether the guest is willing or not.

The Tame Prankster

Once a parrot realizes that he need not be afraid of people but can make good use of them as "substitute parrots," he will delight in playing all kinds of tricks on them. If visitors to our house betray their respect for Vasco's sharp bill, he will often respond by quickly adding a new "buttonhole" to their clothing; and he will keep on repeating his buttonhole trick just to see how far he can push his victim. Sometimes he just pretends to bite, making a snapping noise, and condemns his own misdeed, crying out, "Stop that, you!" The victim will do well to show determined resistance and take a firm hold of the upper mandible of Vasco's bill (that is the mobile portion of the bill). A parrot is quick to notice that he cannot always do just as he pleases, and he will soon leave potential victims in peace.

39

Taming Your Parrot and Adapting Him to His New Home

Pecking Order in the Family

There is only one member of our family who played his cards wrong with Vasco, and that is my father. At first, he was Vasco's favorite human being because he whistled at the bird only from a distance and never came too close. Later, my father made the mistake of protesting loudly whenever Vasco tried out his bill on him. This only encouraged Vasco to bite all the harder; and ever since the time Vasco drew blood from my father's finger, Vasco has taken himself to be the stronger of the two. Then my father made his second mistake. He started to pull his finger away quickly whenever Vasco came near him. Vasco was quick to notice that, and from that point on he took great delight in "Daddy hunts." On one of these "hunts," Vasco climbs up on the back of my father's chair and runs back and forth with his feathers puffed up impressively while my father tries to evade Vasco's bill. Vasco has assumed the higher rank in the pecking order. The rest of us, who do not get bitten, thought Father was exaggerating at first, but we have come to see that he was absolutely right. If Vasco gets hold of any part of my father's anatomy, he does not hesitate to bite down on it. This does not mean, however, that Vasco dis-likes my father. On the contrary, he is very fond of him, as he amply demonstrates by his body language and his enthusiasm for imitating the tunes Father whistles. Vasco has merely established a pecking order: He comes first, then my father.

I have included this episode here to illustrate that parrots do not always express their affection by billing and cooing. Birds are not people, after all, and they express affection in different ways. Then, too, a pecking order of this kind is established in every parrot flock in the wild, and who holds which rank is perfectly clear to every member of the flock. Whether in nature, in an aviary, or in a family, there are always individuals who assume leadership positions and high rankings, and there are others who fill the lower ranks. Indeed, there may even be a "whipping boy"; and if it becomes obvious that one parrot in an aviary is taking a beating, it is a good idea to remove him from the group. In the wild, such a bird could avoid the attacks of the others by simply moving on. But in a flock in captivity, the owner has to see to it that peace reigns.

Daily Routine

The initial period of patient reserve is behind you now. Your parrot leaves his cage and makes short flights around the room. He may even have established a favorite perch on his climbing tree and enjoys watching life go on around him. He becomes friendlier with you day by day, for he has understood that you mean well by him. He happily lets you carry him around everywhere on your shoulder, and he will soon tilt his head toward you, indicating that he would like to have it scratched. It can, of course, take a long time until you reach this stage. I know a parrot that needed a year to become tame.

A Place in the Sun

I have already mentioned that your parrot's cage should not be placed in the direct sunlight. But as long as some shade is available to him, he will

If your parrot becomes absorbed in grooming his feathers, that is a sign that he is content and feels safe.

certainly have no objections to a little warm sunshine. Like you and me, your parrot should be allowed to take a sunbath. The rule of thumb you can apply is that the amount of sun you tolerate comfortably will be right for an acclimatized parrot, too. If he has gotten too hot, a bath or shower will do no harm.

Your Parrot Outdoors

If you have a large yard and the kind of parrot that is a climber by nature, nothing will make your bird happier than long stretches of time spent outdoors in the trees; but be sure to keep an eye on him. Let me take Vasco for an example again. He has a climbing tree on our terrace as well as one in the living room. If the family is sitting on the terrace, he prefers to be with us on his climbing tree. But if we are cutting the grass or doing other outdoor chores, then he likes to do a little "tree pruning" himself, climbing around in the trees and putting his bill to good use. As parrot lovers, we have to put up with the damage he does to the trees. His sharp bill needs wood to work on. I can write about this climbing time on balcony, terrace, or in the yard with equanimity because I know Vasco well, and I know that he will never fly away under any circumstances. But I would urge great caution on other

Daily Routine

parrot owners, and I would not recommend that you adopt my own laissez-faire attitude until you know your own bird so well that you can predict his behavior in any situation. If you do not yet have this kind of confidence, you can set up a safe outdoor area on your balcony or in your yard by making an enclosure out of light wire mesh. If your bird should be frightened unexpectedly, the enclosure will keep him from fluttering over the hedge into your neighbor's yard, where a cat may be waiting for him, or onto the street, where he could be run over. If you can incorporate a tree or some shrubs into your safety enclosure, giving your bird a place to climb, he will be all the more content.

A parrot that is outdoors will go into panic and make unpredictable attempts at flight if he feels threatened by birds of prey. A parrot will be acutely aware of these enemies when we can see no more than a tiny speck in the sky. In his initial terror, even a parrot with clipped wings will try to fly to cover. If he is on a balcony or in a small yard, this panicked flight may well end in serious injury or even death.

There are, of course, parrot enthusiasts who leave their birds at large in the house and yard. This is a wonderfully appealing arrangement for both humans and birds, but it requires courage as well as a large yard in a rural area free of heavy traffic. Konrad Lorenz has written about two parrots, an Amazon and a cockatoo, that he let live free in his house. But then, too, his household contained a number of animal lovers who always had an eye out for the birds' well-being.

The Foot Chain

Unfortunately, the foot chain continues to be used as a method for keeping parrots from flying away. But it is about the worst possible method that can be used, and all true parrot lovers reject it out of hand. The chain has to be attached to the foot with a ring. The combined weight of the ring and chain pull on the foot, cutting into it and often causing serious disorders. Also, the chain has to be quite short or the bird will become tangled in it. The fact that the chain has to be changed over to the other foot at least every two months shows how damaging it is and how much a bird suffers from it.

Clipping the Wings

A life without a chain but always confined to a room is not an acceptable long-term solution for a parrot either, for he has to have unfiltered

Daily Routine

sunlight and should be allowed to go outside, at least during the warm seasons. If you have an outdoor aviary or enclosure you can skip this section; but if your parrot is an indoor pet that lives with you, you will have to find a different solution. Either you can put the caged bird outdoors for a while (if he is primarily a flying bird); or, if your bird is a climber (a macaw, Amazon, African Grey, or cockatoo), you can turn him loose in the trees in your yard. You have to keep an eye on the bird, of course; and as an additional safety measure, you can clip his wings in the summertime. I feel this is unnecessary for an indoor bird in the winter because the cold air that comes in through an open door or window will prompt the bird to pull back from it rather than fly out into it. The only feathers that need to be cut back are the primaries. A veterinarian or pet dealer can clip the wings for you at first. Later, you may want to do it yourself as I do, although I always have the feeling that Vasco will hate me for it. But he does not. On the contrary, once I have finished, he is always particularly hungry for affection; and if I scratch his head, his vexation is soon forgotten. Before you try clipping feathers, you should realize that only six or eight primaries on either side need to be cut and that

they should be cut just a bit above where the quill emerges from the skin. Before you clip, though, make sure that the blood vessels have withdrawn from the quill. If the feathers have not yet reached their full length after a molt, the inner end of the quill will still contain blood vessels, and the blood circulation is still supplying the feathers with necessary nourishment. Cutting into these blood vessels is painful for the bird and causes unnecessary loss of blood. After every molt, then, you have to wait until the feathers reach full length before cutting them back. But during this waiting period, your parrot has his full flight capability, and you will have to be careful that he does not fly away on you. You also have to keep track of feather growth because the primaries can grow back to full length again before the bird goes through his next complete molt.

Should Only One Wing Be Clipped?

Some experts recommend that only one wing be clipped so that the bird loses his balance if he tries to fly. I do not agree with this. If both wings are clipped, the bird can then at least make a few balanced flight movements. I think it is important, too, that the bird still be able to make brief, fluttering flights. If the bird should be endangered, he is still able,

Parrot behavior. Above, left: Biting the neck and ▷
the gesture of submission in response. Above, right:
Drumming with a foot. Below, left: Social
grooming. Below, right: Threatening with a raised
foot.

with some effort, to fly a short distance to safety. I once saw a cockatoo that had both wings clipped come dive-bombing down out of a tree to attack a barking dachshund. The attack went beautifully and had the desired effect on the dog, which pulled back in terror. But then the dachshund counterattacked. The cockatoo could not fly high into the tree, but his frantic flappings got him off the ground enough to reach a low-hanging branch out of the dog's reach.

Grounding a Parrot by Surgery

Another method for keeping a parrot from flying is to cut one or both flight muscles. Let me say that I consider this to be gross cruelty to animals. First, the bird is made incapable of flight for life; and, second, he cannot even flap his wings. Even if a parrot flies or just flutters about rarely indoors, his wings are still important means of locomotion and, frequently, of defense. If they no longer function, the bird is a cripple.

Grooming and Bathing

Grooming feathers is an important activity for all birds, and they can spend hours at it. Parrots are no exception; they do, however, produce more dust in the process than small songbirds do. Cockatoos are particularly notorious for the amounts of "powder" they give off. This powder consists of tiny scales that form as the feather sheaths break up. Each new feather grows in a sheath that does not fall away until the feather has passed through the skin. This is why birds groom themselves so diligently both during and after a molt and why the amount of fine dust is so large at these times. But even the routine smoothing and oiling of the feathers takes a lot of time every day. With movements worthy of a contortionist, the parrot can reach every part of his body and smooth each feather with his bill. Occasionally, he uses his head to take some oil from the uropygial gland. With rubbing motions of the head, he applies the oil to the feathers, then spreads it out with his bill. The only places he cannot reach are his head, the nape of his neck, and underneath his bill. In the wild, his partner would groom these areas for him; and since you are his substitute partner, he asks you to perform this service by scratching these areas for him. This "social grooming" is motivated not only by the bird's need to have his feathers groomed but also by his need for affection, and it is therefore of great importance to his well-being on both accounts.

Clean as your bird may be, he still needs to bathe, too (sometimes sim-

ply to cool off). In his native habitat in the tropics this was a simple matter. It rains often there, and all a parrot has to do if he wants a shower is to sit directly in the storm or under some dripping foliage, or he can bathe in a puddle.

Some parrots, particularly the smaller varieties, like to get right in the water and splash around. For these birds, pet stores carry bath houses that can be hung in the open cage door. If you buy one, be sure it has a corrugated floor so that the bird will not slip in it and fall. For larger parrots, you can use photographers' developing trays as bathtubs. These should be of plastic and have a ribbed floor, too. If a parrot likes a bathtub, he will also like to splash about in it and be able to dip the underside of his wings in the water. Other parrots, such as Grey Parrots and Amazons, prefer showers. For this purpose, you can use a plant sprayer with an atomizer nozzle.

Warning! Never use a plant sprayer that has been used to apply pesticides.

If it is warm both outdoors and in, your bird will want to bathe often, perhaps even twice a day. You will be able to tell that he is too warm because he makes himself very thin and holds his wings away from his

A plant sprayer makes an excellent parrot shower for hygiene and for cooling off on hot days.

body. If I do not respond quickly enough to Vasco's signals, he will begin to complain or splash in his drinking water. Regardless of the time of year, you should offer your parrot a bath or shower at least once a week. If he refuses to have anything to do with water, you should not force baths on him, of course; but keep in mind that for many parrots in captivity it takes a long time to realize that a shower or bath is not dangerous for them but a real pleasure.

Hazards in the Home

Your parrot's curiosity and playfulness can be a source of danger to him, and you will have to keep dangerous objects away from him just as you would for a small child. A tame parrot is extremely curious about everything in his environment, and he is particularly attracted to anything that you happen to be handling. I almost had a heart attack one day

Daily Routine

List of Dangers

Source of Danger	Effects
Drafts from airing the house, open doors and windows	Parrots are very sensitive to drafts, even if the exposure is very brief. Possible results: Colds, inflammation of the crop, pneumonia.
Direct sunlight, overheated room	If the bird cannot get into the shade, he may die of heart failure.
Sudden changes in temperature	Most "house parrots" can tolerate room temperatures between 40 and 75 °F (5–24 °C). However, the bird should be allowed to adjust to new temperatures gradually.
Drawers, cupboards	A curious parrot likes to explore open drawers and cabinets. If he is accidentally shut inside, he can starve to death or suffocate.
Kitchen	Steam and heat from cooking can suffocate a bird. An overheated room that is then aired can produce colds. A parrot can scald himself or drown in open pots containing hot liquids. Hot stove burners: Burns, death from burns. Household cleansers: Poisoning.
Bathroom	Window open for ventilation: Bird escapes. Cleansers and chemicals: Poisoning.
Window panes, picture windows, glass walls	Bird flies into them: Concussion, fractured skull or neck.
Doors	Bird gets caught in them and is crushed.
Containers with water in them (buckets, vases, bowls)	Bird falls in and drowns. Bird can mistake foam on the surface as a firm landing place.
Sinks and tubs filled with water	Drowning.
Ovens, electrical appliances	Burns, death from burns.
Electrical wires and sockets	Shock from biting through wires.
Large decorative vases	Bird can slip in and not be able to climb out again: suffocation, starvation, heart failure. (Fill these containers with sand or paper.)
Knitted or crocheted articles	The bird's toes can get entangled; bird can get trapped and strangle himself.
Yarn, string, chains	Entanglement, strangulation.

Daily Routine

Hard floors	Birds without full powers of flight can break a leg or bruise themselves in a hard landing.
Cage or aviary mesh with wrong sized openings	Bird sticks his head out through the mesh or between bars, gets caught, suffers injury, or possibly strangles to death.
Wire mesh that is too fine or sharp	Cuts on head and feet.
Perches too small in diameter	Excessive growth of toenails, chondrosis.
Sharp objects, nails, splinters, ends of wire	Cuts, puncture wounds.
Human feet	Bird gets stepped on.
Easy chairs, couches	Bird crushed when accidentally sat on.
Poisons	Deadly poisons: lead, verdigris, rust, pans coated with plastics, all household cleansers, mercury. Harmful substances: pencil leads, inserts for ballpoint pens and magic markers, alcohol, coffee, hot spices.
Pesticides	Anything that kills insects or parasites is lethal for your bird. Never spray plants in the room where your bird is kept or bring sprayed plants into that room.
Poisonous plants	Yew, narcissus, primroses.
Nicotine	Smoke-laden air is harmful; nicotine, lethal.
Mites and other parasites	Disinfect cage, toys, areas the bird frequents. Never dust or spray your bird. You may suffocate or poison him. In cases of parasite infestation, consult your veterinarian.
Other house pets	Parrot and dog: Take care in getting your parrot and dog acquainted with each other. Never leave them alone together at first. Parrot and cat: No! Parrot and rabbit, hamster, or guinea pig: Yes, but avoid direct contact. Parrot and fish: Yes, but keep the aquarium covered to prevent bird from drowning in it.

Daily Routine

when I came back to my room after having answered the telephone and found Manaos at work there. I had been getting ready for a trip before I went to the phone and had been in the process of packing my toilet kit. Manaos had been intrigued by this, and to keep him entertained, I had given him a little cardboard box. When I came back into the room, I saw that he had found another plaything: a box of sleeping tablets. He had already taken several tablets out of their aluminum-foil wrapper. Horrified, I snatched the box away from him. Manaos complained loudly, for he had been enjoying the crackling sound the aluminum foil made. A trip to the veterinarian proved unnecessary because all Manaos had done was to take the pills out of the wrapper. Finding they were bitter, he had

not eaten any. Parrots have taste buds on their tongues that usually signal quite reliably that something is inedible. But let my experience be a warning: Medications, household cleansers, and other poisonous substances have to be kept out of a parrot's reach. Not all of them will have a bad taste that will prevent a bird from eating them.

Electrical wires are a major source of danger. A parrot can bite through them in no time at all, and none should be left exposed in areas your parrot frequents.

And you have to be constantly on the alert to see that no doors or windows are left open.

Study the list of dangers on pages 48–49 and take the necessary steps to eliminate these dangers from your home.

Hot burners on the stove are a hazard. Never leave your bird alone in the kitchen.

Electrical wires are a hazard. Make sure your parrot always has fresh branches on which he can gnaw to his heart's content.

The Proper Diet

No parrot can thrive without the proper food, and more often than not scruffy plumage is the consequence of an inadequate diet. Parrots are primarily herbivorous, but occasionally — and this is usually during brooding — they will eat animal foods, too. In the wild, these foods consist mainly of insects and small worms. In captivity, animal protein is usually supplied through hard-boiled eggs and worms. In their native habitat, parrots eat all the plants around them that are to their taste; and a bird in the wild will forage intensively for fruits, bark, plants, bulbs, seeds, nuts, berries, pollen, and, perhaps, for insects and worms as well. In captivity, he has to take what is offered him.

Prepared Foods

The proper seed mixtures for large and small parrots are commercially available. The firms that produce these prepared foods buy exotic seeds in the countries parrots come from and supplement them with local ones. Depending on whether a mixture is meant for large or small parrots, it will contain black or white sunflower seeds, canary seed, millet, oats, wheat, linseed, corn, and nuts. This mixture will be your bird's staple food. Mixes are enriched with minerals, honey, meat, biscuit, liver, oils, iodine, and the major vitamins; and they duplicate by and large what the bird would get in the wild.

The label on the package will tell you for which birds a particular mixture is designed. Note the date stamped on the package, too. Properly stored grains will retain their nutritive value, with some minimal loss, for up to a year after harvest; and they can still be used up to two years.

Important! Do not use these mixes as a basic food for a lory or any large parrot. They feed only on soft foods and should get only some seeds as a supplementary food (see page 52).

After you have had a chance to observe your parrot for a while, you will soon know what he likes best by seeing which food containers he empties first. Make up his menu according to his wishes. If he prefers white sunflower seeds over black, then white ones are what he should have. These supplementary seeds can be bought loose at seed stores. The food dish should then be filled half with these white sunflower seeds and half with a mix. This way your bird will get the basic things he needs for good nutrition. Your bird's tastes may change after a few days or weeks, and you can adjust accordingly. Every now and then you can blow away the shells. Parrots are very adept at shelling seeds, and they let the empty shells fall where they may. As a rule,

The Proper Diet

the shells land in the food container and cover up the uneaten seeds.

And of course your parrot should get fresh water every day. Be sure to rinse his water dish, as well as his food dish, with hot water each time you refill it.

Prepared foods provide your bird with important nutrients such as protein, fats, carbohydrates, minerals, and some vitamins. But he needs more variety than these foods alone supply.

Fruit and Vegetables

Pet stores offer various packaged food supplements, such as vitamin drops. These things can certainly help keep your parrot healthy, but I would advise against the excessive use of artificial supplements. What a parrot needs, preferably every day, in addition to his seed mixture is fruit and vegetables. Offer your parrot different ones to see what he prefers. Here is a list of foods you can try:

Vegetables: Fresh peas in the pod, kohlrabi, fresh corn, carrots, radishes, tomatoes, spinach, lettuce, and mango leaves.

Herbs and wild greens: Parsley, dandelion greens, chickweed, clover, and other garden herbs.

Fruit: Apples, bananas, berries from mountain ash and hawthorn, pears, strawberries, rose hips, raspberries, cherries, kiwis, tangerines, sweet oranges, and grapes.

Nuts: Peanuts, shelled or unshelled; shelled hazel nuts; walnuts both with and without shells; Brazil nuts with or without shells. In the fall, fresh acorns, chestnuts, horse chestnuts.

Be sure to give your parrot only fresh foods of the same quality that you would give your family. Wilted or rotten fruits and vegetables are as bad for animals as they are for people. You should not give your bird anything straight out of the refrigerator; all foods should be fed at room temperature. Vegetables, fruit, and herbs for your parrot should be prepared as for your own table: carefully washed, then rubbed or dripped dry. Your fruit and vegetables should preferably not come from a hothouse, and in no case should they have been sprayed with any chemicals.

Other Supplementary Foods

In addition to fruits and vegetables, many parrots like seeds from grasses, plantain, shepherd's purse, cornflowers, calendula, pansies, and forget-me-nots. Grasses, herbs, and seeds that you collect yourself should be picked only in areas far enough away from roads and highways so that the plants will not be contami-

The Proper Diet

nated by automobile exhausts. These contaminants cannot be removed by simply washing the plants.

Although some parrot experts advise against it, I give Vasco some unseasoned meat occasionally, either raw or cooked. He pounces on meat, poultry, and fish with great glee. He does not get much, of course; as a rule all he gets is what he can gnaw off a leftover chop bone or soup bone. But it clearly is not doing him any harm, for Vasco has such splendid plumage that other parrot owners are green with envy when they see him. One writer observed that his Amazons, Pink Cockatoos, and Palm Cockatoos had such a good appetite for meat that they would even search the dirt floor of their aviary for worms.

Sprouts

Sprouts cannot be found in nature very often, but this valuable supplementary food is easy to produce oneself. All the seeds contained in prepared mixes can be sprouted. Whenever viable seeds absorb water, chemical reactions that bring about sprouting begin to take place in the seeds. This makes their available vitamins, minerals, and trace elements accessible and adds to their nutritive value. Moist, swollen seeds are more nutritious than dry ones, but sprouts are even more valuable. Sprouts are particularly useful in encouraging a pair of breed birds to mate, and they are good to give to any parrot from time to time, especially if fresh fruit and vegetables are in short supply.

This is how you make sprouts. Soften about a teaspoonful of seeds in a little water. The seeds should be covered by about an inch (2 cm) of water. Let the seeds stand for twenty-four hours; then put them in a sieve, spray them thoroughly, and place them in a small, shallow bowl. Cover the bowl with glass or cellophane wrap, and let the seeds sit for another twenty-four to forty-eight hours. After twenty-four hours they can be served as softened seeds; after forty-eight hours, they will be sprouts.

Important: Swollen or sprouted seeds spoil quickly. Give them to your bird in the morning in an extra feeding dish; then, about noon,

Nuts are often a favorite food for parrots. With their feet, they carry nuts to their bills, which they then use to crack the shells.

The Proper Diet

remove what the bird has not yet eaten. This precautionary measure will prevent your parrot from eating sprouts that have begun to go bad and so can prevent illness. After a while, you will learn exactly what the right quantity of sprouts for your bird is.

And here is a special tip: If you have trouble sprouting seeds from your prepared mix, go to a health-food store and buy oats or wheat specially intended for sprouting. If these seeds are stored in a cool, dark, well-ventilated place, you will be able to sprout them easily even a year later.

Wood and Bark

The fresh branches of all non-poisonous trees and shrubs are important for your parrot not only as gymnastic apparatus, resting place, and workroom but also as a source of valuable nutrients. Parrots like to gnaw on and eat wood and bark that contains carbohydrates, iron, copper, trace elements, and vitamins. Since it is a major project to change the large branches of your parrot's climbing tree, make a point of bringing back twigs from your walk. Your parrot will soon reduce them to small chips. Parrots are particularly fond of lilac, willow, oak, alder, poplar, beech, mountain ash, elder, and hazel nut, also of twigs and blossoms from fruit

trees. Be sure, however, that the fruit trees have not been sprayed.

Calcium Requirements

Calcium is an important nutrient that every bird needs in the regeneration of its feathers, bill, and toenails as well as for strengthening the bones; and every opportunity for meeting the bird's calcium requirements should be taken. The grit or gravel on the bottom of the bird's cage serves the same kind of double function that twigs and branches do, for the grit contains calcium. However, this source alone is not adequate. The grains of grit the bird eats assist the digestion process in the stomach in addition to providing some calcium. Do not use just any sand you can find outdoors as litter for your parrot's cage because it will not have been cleaned and may well carry infections or parasites. You can avoid these dangers if you buy prepackaged bird grit.

Your parrot should also have a mineral stone in his cage. This stone provides the additional calcium your bird needs as well as serving as a whetstone for his bill. Pet stores have these stones available in different sizes. They are a mixture of finely crushed limestone, seashells, phosphate rock, and quartz grit; and they also contain iodine, iron, and other

The Proper Diet

trace elements. Instead of a mineral stone, you can use cuttlebone or seashells. These can be bought in pet stores, or you can collect them yourself at the seashore.

Since not every parrot is enthusiastic about gnawing on a mineral stone, cuttlebone, or seashells, it is a good idea to scatter a fine thin layer of powdered calcium over your bird's food every day. You can buy preparations such as Avitron or Nekton, which contain vitamins A, E, C, D, niacin, B_1, B_2, B_4, and B_{12}, and some minerals.

Spoil Your Parrot, within Limits

Not every parrot will delight in all the foods I have listed here. Always offer your bird a variety of foods and particularly the ones he likes best. Do not leave leftover perishables, like fruit, vegetables, herbs, meat, and sprouts, within his reach for long. Spoiled foods can be harmful.

Do not give your bird a diet of nothing but seeds simply to avoid the mess that soft foods make. On pages 57–58 I suggest some quick and easy methods for cleaning up after your parrot's sloppy meals. Do not impose a monotonous diet on your parrot; for he, like us, eats not only to keep himself alive but also for enjoyment.

Do not hold it against him if he repeatedly spurns foods that you have gone to some trouble and expense to get. Either he will have to develop a taste for a certain food gradually, or he may have an unshakeable aversion for it.

A cockatoo I took care of once seemed determined to starve to death rather than accept grains in place of the sunflower seeds he preferred. So I yielded to his wishes and gave him sunflower seeds.

One final note: Do not be sparing with the basic feed of mixed seeds. A parrot that is kept busy will not overeat out of boredom. But his metabolism is such that he needs to take small portions often. These should be available to him in the accustomed place at all times, and he should be able to choose as he likes among a wide variety of seeds.

Water for Your Parrot

Be sure that the water dish is always clean, and give your parrot fresh, cool (but not ice cold) water at least twice a day. If the water is dirty, change it right away. If your parrot was just recently imported, he should get only boiled water at body temperature at first. Or you can give him a special bird beverage available at pet stores. This beverage is recommended if you live in an area where the drinking water is of poor quality.

Pet stores also sell drops that contain vitamins and agents that disinfect

The Proper Diet

the water, and it is a good idea to put these in your bird's water in accordance with the directions on the package. If your bird is getting enough vitamins and minerals from his food, then three drops of vitamin liquid per week are enough. If his intake of fruit and vegetables is small, give him three drops each day.

Table Manners

If a parrot starts to eat somewhere in your living room and not in his cage, the spectacle is enough to drive one to distraction. His manners are much better adapted to the jungle than they are to a civilized household. Only a fraction of what he takes into his bill actually lands in his digestive tract, and bits of ripe fruit, nutshells, and other food particles land on the floor. All you can do to cope with this is to lay a floor covering under his eating place (see page 57).

Food as a Plaything

Eating provides parrots not only with nourishment but also with an opportunity for play. Vasco, for example, who is far from atypical in this, prefers cherries with stems to those without. And he takes a lot of time preparing his cherries just the way he likes them. After much twisting and turning, he nips the stem off so that he can get at the fruit itself.

But then he may not eat the cherry. He may have his heart set on using the pit as a new toy, or he may just suck the juice, squirting it all around him in the process. What is left, sucked more or less dry, he either lets fall to the floor or throws away. A nut, too, can be both food and toy. No matter how hard the nutshell, a parrot will know how to cope with it. Do not be too quick to deprive a large parrot of the pleasures of nut-cracking if he does not manage to crack a shell instantly. Even a macaw, which can crack any nut with ease, likes to prolong the work of nut-cracking. He turns the hard nut over and over, searching for a vulnerable point in it. Usually he will find one. If not, he will scrape at one place with his bill until the nut is worn thin enough to crack. The underside of the upper mandible is equipped with "filing notches" that fill this very purpose, and this probing and experimenting with a nut

While breaking up his food with his pincer-like bill, a parrot tests it with his tongue to see if it tastes good.

The Proper Diet

is an important activity: Because the horn-like bill continues to grow, it has to be constantly worn down on hard objects.

A parrot also likes to share in the meals of his "family." Vasco knows exactly when mealtime is, and if a meal is delayed for some reason, he starts to grumble. He is not interested in the food alone but also in the company mealtimes afford. If we do not go get him and set him on the back of a chair, he will waddle over himself and climb up someone's pants or chair leg to take his place on the back of a chair. Then comes his inevitable question: "What?" If we do not respond immediately, he will ask louder, "Well, what?" And this question rises to a crescendo if we continue to ignore him. At some point, we give in. He never does, and so he gets his "what" to eat. If the "what" does not suit him, he will toss it onto the rug, and we have to supply another "what." When he is satisfied with his "what," he then devours it with pleasure. If we are eating asparagus, he shows a marked preference for the tips!

A Parrot Is a Messy Companion!

That is, unfortunately, a fact of life with parrots. The cleverer a parrot is, the more playful he will be and the more eager to keep busy. Only if he is left alone will he vegetate and sink into lethargy, for social animals are used to doing what their comrades do. A healthy, active parrot will spend a lot of time keeping his bill busy. The traces of this activity will land on the floor, and the end products of his digestion land there, too. In eating soft fruits, he will squirt the juice; and he will toss the remains of both fruit and seeds onto the floor. He also sheds feathers and gives off clouds of fine dust when he shakes himself or puffs out his feathers. It would be cruel to keep him constantly caged to avoid the mess these perfectly normal processes cause.

Hygienic Measures You Can Take

Sheets of builder's polyethylene film are invaluable in keeping parrot-caused chaos under control. If you put a piece of this plastic sheeting on the wall behind your parrot's cage, sprayed fruit juices can easily be wiped away.

A similar sheet can be spread on the floor under the cage and under the climbing tree to spare your carpet. Again, the plastic can be easily cleaned with a damp cloth, and it looks a lot better on your floor than a scattering of old newspapers.

The Proper Diet

Sandbox

If you have your climbing tree not only in a Christmas tree stand or bucket but in a sandbox or tub as well then you can do without the plastic sheet on the floor, provided the branches of the tree do not extend beyond the outer limits of the sandbox. For the sake of economy, fill the box or tub up as high as you like with gravel, then spread a thin layer of bird grit over the gravel. This should be packaged bird grit from the pet store, for your bird will probably peck at this grit, and he should not be exposed to the parasites or infections that unwashed grit might contain. Check the tub every day, scooping out droppings and dirty areas with an old spoon you keep for this purpose. Spread a new layer of grit as needed.

Parrots Cannot Be Housebroken

Your parrot can never be housebroken, and he will let something drop quite often. As fliers, birds are quick to empty the cloaca so that they will not have to carry about any unnecessary ballast. Fortunately, seed-eating birds produce relatively firm feces. Among parrots, the lories are among the few varieties that live almost exclusively on fruit.

It does not make me particularly nervous when Vasco sits on my shoulder or knee. In the wild, he would not dirty his own nest; and in captivity, he does not dirty me. He always makes the effort to hold out as long as he can, and then if he has reached his limit, he is considerate enough to let his droppings fall past my knee or shoulder. But even with his best efforts, accidents do happen. When and if they do, droppings should be wiped off smooth surfaces right away with a damp cloth. On textiles, droppings can be washed out easily with water.

Cleanliness Is Crucial

The same diligence that you bring to cleaning up after your parrot in your home has to be applied to your parrot's cage, climbing tree, food dishes, perches, and toys. Wherever droppings fall they should be cleaned up immediately, if possible, and, if not, then at least once a day, using warm water. Droppings that have hardened on wooden surfaces should be removed with a little scraper that you can buy in your pet store for this purpose. Then the spot should be washed. Spoon out droppings and dirt from the grit in the bottom of the cage every day, and wash food and water containers in hot water daily. At least once a week you should wash the floor and the floor tray of the cage in the bathtub with water as hot as you can stand to use. Scrub with a brush, then rinse clean. Every four to six weeks, the entire cage should receive this same treatment.

If Your Parrot Is Sick

Once a parrot has adapted to his new surroundings, he is not prone to illness if properly cared for. He can, of course, have a minor illness now and then—a cold or slight diarrhea—but this should be no cause for worry. If, however, your parrot seems seriously ill, you should consult your veterinarian right away. Even for a veterinarian it can sometimes be difficult to arrive at a conclusive diagnosis and so to prescribe the correct treatment on the first try. My main reason for describing here the major illnesses parrots can get is to make your consultations with your veterinarian easier and more productive. Also, I would like to help you to recognize illness quickly.

The major general symptoms of illness are apathy or any other noticeable change in behavior; difficulty in breathing; red or inflamed eyes; loss of appetite; diarrhea, possibly with unusually colored droppings; rough plumage or loss of feathers; wounds; incrustations on the skin, bill, or feet. Since many serious illnesses can be diagnosed from the droppings, be sure to take a sample with you when you go to the veterinarian. To collect it, put a piece of non-absorbent paper under your parrot's sleeping place overnight.

Before you read about the individual diseases, study the drawing "Parrot Anatomy" on page 7. Your consultation with your veterinarian will be easier if you know the correct terms for all the parts of your parrot's body.

When a parrot is sick, he will lie on his perch more than sit on it; his feathers will be ruffled, his eyes half closed.

Parrot Fever (Psittacosis)

This is the best known of parrot diseases. It is a virus infection, which is by no means limited to parrots; and for this reason it is also known as ornithosis or bird fever. This disease should be reported to public health authorities because human beings can be infected by it. The infection can be passed on to humans by fecal particles carried in the air. Parrots can be carriers of the disease without becoming ill from it. Parrots in quarantine are treated with chlortetracyclin for a period of 30 days. As a result, ornithosis carried by parrots has become quite rare. Healthy birds that have no contact with infected birds run practically no chance of contracting this disease. In human beings, ornithosis

59

If Your Parrot Is Sick

resembles a persistent flu or typhus, often in conjunction with pneumonia. It can be successfully treated with antibiotics.

The symptoms of the disease in parrots are not particularly easy to detect. The bird may have difficulty in breathing, noisy breathing, crop inflammation, and cramps or paralysis. Almost all birds that are ill with psittacosis sit around apathetically with their feathers fluffed up and will not eat.

Newcastle Disease

This virus infection is an atypical bird disease. It is infectious for parrots but not for people. In parrots, it is fatal. There is no cure. Conjunctivitis, diarrhea, colds, and unusual movements can be symptoms of Newcastle disease. If these symptoms appear, the bird's fate is already sealed.

Parasites

Parasites can be carried in sand, dirt, plants, or other things that come from outside sources and have not been cleaned. The soil in a dirt-floored aviary may also contain them.

You should watch out for parasites, too, if you acquire new birds. Keep the newcomers isolated for about four weeks before you put them together with any bird or birds you already have.

Worms (Endoparasites)

Infestations with worms are tricky because they can easily escape notice. To all appearances, the birds seem to be healthy; and only if they are affected by some other disorder, such as an otherwise harmless cold or a temporary vitamin deficiency, does the worm infection become acute. The bird is then no longer able to tolerate the parasites and becomes obviously ill. The most common endoparasites in parrots are the roundworm (*Ascaridia*) and the hairworm (*Capillaria*). Roundworms and hairworms occur in the digestive tract, primarily in the small intestine, causing bleeding and, consequently, brownish droppings. Unfortunately, the symptoms rarely permit a conclusive diagnosis. If you suspect a worm infestation, take a sample of droppings to the veterinarian for examination.

If your bird should become infected with worms, his cage has to be disinfected and his climbing tree replaced with a new one. If worms occur in aviary birds, the aviary floor will be infested and will have to be thoroughly cleaned and disinfected. Wolfgang de Grahl recommends going over the floor with high-powered

If Your Parrot Is Sick

blowtorches and, if the floor is of dirt, replacing it with a new layer. With a dirt floor, you have to be sure to keep out earthworms. The earthworms take in the infected droppings from the birds, and the parrots become reinfected by eating these earthworms. Appropriate disinfectants are available at pet stores.

Mites (Ectoparasites)

The red bird mite (*Dermanyssus avium*) is the most common of the mites that attack birds by sucking their blood. If the infestation is heavy, the bird will become anemic from it, and young birds can die of it. Mites can also carry other diseases. This parasite spends the daytime hours hidden in cracks and corners near the bird, sucking its blood during the night. Cage, perches, nesting box, and any other places or objects the bird uses should be cleaned with appropriate disinfectants. The disinfectants have to be used repeatedly because the mite eggs cannot be destroyed with only one application. The affected bird should be carefully dusted with a safe anti-mite powder. Be careful when you dust the bird that no powder gets in his eyes, nostrils, or open bill. While the red mite attacks the bird's entire body, the burrowing mite (*Cnemidocoptesc*) is found mainly on the feet, causing a chalky coating there, hence the name

"scaly leg" for an infestation of this kind. A mite-killing oil or salve may be used on the legs. This same treatment can be used for mites that produce an incrustation on the bill. Another parasite is the relatively harmless but ugly feather mite (*Mallophaga*) that feeds on the bird's feathers and makes the plumage look rough, even powdery. For a heavy infestation of these mites, have your veterinarian recommend an appropriate medication.

Fungus Infections (Mycoses)

Two kinds of fungus infection (*Aspergillus fumigatus* and *Candida albicans*) can attack the respiratory organs, the throat, and, especially, the crop and the bill. As a rule, nothing can be detected with the naked eye. Affected areas may be swollen, and the bird will have difficulty in breathing. This fungus is spread primarily by spoiled food. The veterinarian has to catch the disease early; otherwise there is little he can do, and the illness — especially if it is caused by *Aspergillus* — will be fatal. Skin mycoses are less serious than those affecting internal organs, and the veterinarian can treat them with salves and solutions. Symptoms of an internal fungus infection are apathy, loss of appetite, passing of a cloudy and often brownish slime mixed with

Two macaws supplementing their mineral intake, ▷
photographed in the jungles of Peru by Walter
Dossenbach.

seeds, sometimes diarrhea and shortness of breath. At the first sign of
these symptoms consult your veterinarian immediately. These symptoms
can also occur with a crop inflammation that is caused by a different
agent and that can be cured easily if it
is treated early enough. Parasites that
attack external areas cause visible
changes or noticeable changes in
behavior. With mites, the bird will be
restless, particularly at night. When
he should be sleeping quietly, he will
instead be constantly and nervously
probing about in his feathers with his
bill.

Colds

The signs of colds are inflamed
eyes, reddishness around the eyes,
and swelling of the eyelids. Newly imported birds that are not yet acclimated are particularly susceptible to
colds, but colds develop into the
more serious pneumonia much less
often than is commonly believed.
Still, it is better to be safe than sorry,
for eye inflammations and shortness
of breath are often accompanying
symptoms of serious diseases. In any
case, a parrot with these symptoms
should be kept in a draft-free room
with a constant temperature of about
75 °F (24 °C). Do not feed any cold
foods, and offer the bird lukewarm

camomile tea to drink. Careful use of
an infrared heat lamp can help speed
recovery.

Diarrhea

Except among the fruit-eaters, such
as lories, parrot droppings are usually
quite firm and have white and green
components. The droppings can, of
course, show other coloration for
reasons other than disease. A large
meal of cherries or blueberries, for
example, will color the droppings.
That is clearly no cause for alarm.
Only if diarrhea persists for several
days and the droppings remain dis-
colored should you suspect some kind
of disorder. Since diarrhea accom-
panies many diseases, you should
consult your veterinarian about it. A
routine case of diarrhea caused by the
wrong foods or spoiled foods can be
treated by use of the heat lamp and
by feeding baby food, boiled rice,
weak black tea, and hard-boiled eggs.
The bird should also get ample water
because he will lose a lot of fluid
through the diarrhea.

This is the way to apply a wing bandage if a wing bone is broken.

Cutting the toenails. Left, wrong; right, correct. Be careful not to cut into the quick of the nail.

Egg Binding in Females

Parrots rarely suffer from egg binding because they do not often breed in captivity. Also, it is difficult to detect egg binding because the female is in her nesting box and should not be disturbed. The symptoms of egg binding: The female raises her tail feathers, presses her eyes shut, and bears down as though she were trying to pass droppings. You can and should help by gently massaging the belly downwards toward the cloaca and by keeping the bird very warm. This will, of course, somewhat frighten a parrot that is not completely tame. If you have to take the bird to the veterinarian, be sure to keep her warm on the way.

Feather Plucking

Feather plucking is a parrot "disease" that is not yet fully understood, but we do know that this disorder is psychic in origin and is comparable to

Overgrowth of Toenails and Bill

Parrots in captivity often do not have enough opportunity to wear down their toenails and bills. If your parrot can spend as much time as he likes on his climbing tree, this is less likely; but you still have to watch for excessive growth and have overly long nails and bills cut back. Have a dealer or veterinarian do this for you, for there is a chance that you might cut back too far, causing bleeding and pain to your bird.

You will notice when your bird's toenails are too long. He may, for example, get them caught in the carpet. If the upper mandible grows out too far beyond the lower one, the bird will have trouble eating. A preventive measure here is to feed your bird hard nuts and hard woods.

If Your Parrot Is Sick

nail biting in humans. Veterinarians and ornithologists think some of the causes of feather plucking are lack of activity (boredom), vitamin or mineral deficiencies, psychoses evoked by incompatible pairing or by the lack of a partner, and excessively dry air in rooms with central heating. For whatever reason, a feather plucker will begin to pull out a few feathers or bite them off. The disorder will have

then he should be given a tree with fresh bark on it. If the air is too dry, get a humidifier. In their native habitat, parrots are usually accustomed to tropical heat and humidity and it is not surprising that they find our centrally heated air much too dry. And, last but not least, provide your bird with more vitamins and a highly varied diet including nuts that have to be cracked.

A "feather plucker." Common causes of this self-mutilation are boredom and lack of freedom to move about.

run its course when the bird simply decides himself to stop or when he is completely naked. Some parrots will stop if they are given a climbing tree to occupy them, if their diet is changed, or if they are given a partner.

First Aid: A feather plucker needs to be kept busy. If he has either no climbing tree or only a worn out one,

Keeping Your Parrot Occupied

In the wild, parrots have a lot of companionship (see page 73) and keep their powerful bills busy all the time; and in captivity, too, a parrot has to have plenty of work for his bill. As long as a parrot has his climbing tree, branches with bark on them, and other objects like nuts, corks, and appropriate toys that he can either crack or gnaw on, he will do little damage to your home. All parrot keepers who, like me, have become wise through experience know how important fresh climbing trees with bark on them are in keeping a parrot well occupied.

Protecting Your Home

If Vasco wants to try out his bill on other objects, whether wallpaper or furniture, I either cover the object of his interest or try to turn him away from it with a kind of "scarecrow." To protect the wallpaper, for instance, I cover it temporarily with old newspapers. If he is drawn to the back of an upholstered chair, I cover it with a cloth. If this approach fails, I put something that Vasco dislikes in the vulnerable spot. That keeps him away, and after a while the "scarecrow" can be removed because Vasco has long since turned his attentions to some new target.

Scolding Is of No Use

It is useless to scold or punish a parrot and tends to make him angry and more unmanageable. Try outsmarting him instead. Divert his attention by playing with some other object. Like a child, he will soon want to play with the same thing you are playing with. You can also divert him by giving him a cardboard box, a cork, or some other dispensable object to destroy.

Toys for Your Parrot

Whenever I have something in my hand—slides, a ball-point pen, or a cork—Vasco will want to have it, too. Whenever I want to write now, I always have an extra ball-point (without the magazine in it) ready for Vasco. I used to worry at first that he might swallow something that would harm him, but not a single particle ever went down his throat. All his scraps landed on the floor. But still, for safety's sake, it is best to give your parrot toys made of cork, wood, leather, or sisal. Pet stores and the pet sections of department stores carry toys especially designed for parrots, such as indestructible mirrors, bells, wooden dolls, and sisal cords. All you have to do to interest your parrot in a toy is to play with it

Keeping Your Parrot Occupied

yourself for a while. The most important thing in a toy is that your parrot be able to take it apart. Corks from wine bottles are among Vasco's favorite toys. The minute he sees a wine bottle brought into the room he begins to get impatient, for he has learned that where there are wine bottles, there are also corks. And as social creatures, parrots always like those things best that their "companions" are using or playing with.

Drawers and Closets as Caves

Open drawers are a source of great delight to many parrots. And if the drawers happen to be stuffed full of all sorts of odds and ends, it makes a high holiday for a parrot to paw around in what he finds, sort it, and toss things out. This is all harmless enough, but you should be sure there is nothing in the drawer that might harm your parrot, also that he does not get accidentally closed up in the drawer. It is only natural that parrots like these substitute caves because in the wild they nest in hollows. Our Vasco likes these "hollow trees," too, and he fluffs himself up in them with great pleasure. He nods his head vigorously to show his pleasure over my visit, and he would no doubt like it if he could build a nest with me.

That I am too big to fit into his cave seems to escape his attention altogether. But I do the best I can, playing around with my hand in his cave and, of course, scratching his head a bit.

Parrots are great climbers and acrobats. This drawing shows an African Grey doing a forward roll on an index finger. He uses his bill to pull himself up on the other side.

Keeping Your Parrot Occupied

Mirror, Mirror on the Wall

The experts disagree on whether a parrot should have a mirror or not. In my opinion, it is impossible to prevent your bird from seeing his reflected image occasionally, either in polished furniture, a window pane, or in a mirror. I drew the logical conclusion from this and got a mirror for Vasco.

Pet stores have unbreakable mirrors made of heavy, polished metal. Vasco plays with his a lot, does gymnastics on it, beats it with his wings, climbs on it, sits next to it—and often ignores it. I have never had the impression that he takes the image he sees in the mirror for a partner or a rival. A different parrot might behave differently, of course, but judging from my experience a mirror does no harm.

The Pleasure of Your Company

For a single parrot, the people around him take the place of other parrots, and he insists on being in their company. If you go into another room, your parrot may want to be taken along. After all, parrots in the wild do everything in company, too. Many parakeets follow their owners on the wing. The species that do not fly so well like to be taken along on someone's shoulder. Vasco always insists on riding on my shoulder no matter where I go. If he sees that I am about to leave the room, he draws his feathers in close to him and shakes all over, especially with his wings. He looks as helpless as a very young bird; and, in addition to his gestures, he adds the clearly stated question, "Well, what now?" Then I offer him my shoulder, and he climbs on. He expresses his satisfaction by nodding his head energetically.

How Parrots Learn to Talk

Scientific study of parrot behavior is still a long way from understanding parrots fully, but this much we do know: In the wild, parrots do not tend to imitate sounds foreign to their species; and studies made to date indicate that they do not do it even if they live near human habitations and hear different sounds quite a lot.

Imitation of sounds appears to be something parrots in captivity do to keep busy and avoid boredom. The single parrot that necessarily orients himself to human beings tries to find some way to communicate with his human partner. In doing so, he learns to imitate not only words and sentences but also sounds prevalent in

Keeping Your Parrot Occupied

his environment. But the ability to imitate varies not only from species to species but from bird to bird. One may talk a blue streak while another can manage only a few meager syllables. But all parrots can learn something. Still, a parrot owner should not be excessively concerned about his bird's ability to speak, for many an inarticulate parrot can still make an affectionate and amusing pet.

To teach even the most gifted parrot to talk, you will have to repeat the same words over and over again. Start with only a few words. One person should do all the teaching, speaking the chosen words quietly, in the same tone of voice, and only when the bird is really listening. Once the ice is broken and your bird has learned one word, others will follow. Your parrot will then add to his vocabulary quickly, sometimes using it appropriately, sometimes not.

Vasco's repertoire is quite large now; and as many Grey Parrots do, he often uses what he has learned at the right time and in the right place. Early in the morning, for example, he will say, "Good morrrrrning." At night, he produces a very clear, "Good night, Papa." He has never confused morning and night. Or he may demand, "Scratch, come scratch!," nodding his head in a typical gesture of body language.

This behavior would suggest that Vasco knows what he is saying, but in actuality we are probably witnessing a process of association. Certain sounds are associated with certain situations. Teaching him was easy. Whenever I scratched his head, I would repeat, "Scratch, come scratch!" The same approach was used to teach him "Good morning." We have also been successful in teaching Vasco to reprimand himself whenever he bites holes in the furniture. He says "Stop that!" to himself, and this has the advantage for us of letting us know in good time that he is up to mischief.

Vasco uses his vocabulary with other animals, too. He once tried to scare off a bumblebee with the words: "Stop that."

Some parrots will learn not only to use their words at the right time but also to anticipate what is to come. In the evening, for example, when we are getting ready for bed, Vasco will say "Good night, Papa" incessantly. He knows that it is just about bedtime. He will almost always anticipate sequences of events that he has observed often enough. And sometimes he will use his "Good night" routine to set things in motion if he wants to go to sleep but we have not yet made any preparations for bed. Then he will keep on saying "Good night,

Keeping Your Parrot Occupied

Papa" until we take the hint and disappear.

Imitating Sounds and Movements

Almost all parrot species like to whistle tunes. One may imitate an entire song; another, only a few phrases. All parrots can make music, and they like to, sitting on the highest branch of their climbing tree.

They also like to imitate movements. Amazons and cockatoos as well as Grey Parrots have this talent. Cockatoos can be so comical in their movements that they have been called "feathered monkeys." They do gymnastics, dance, rock back and forth, and do the most outlandish tricks on their climbing trees. If you reward these performances with hearty laughter, your bird will feel encouraged to outdo himself.

If I dance to radio music, Vasco will make similar motions. If I nod my head, he takes a bow, too. If I reach for a damp cloth to clean up his droppings, then he will scrub with his bill at whatever he is standing on.

Understanding Parrots

Parrots are creatures of the wild that come to us with the behavior of wild creatures. It may help you to understand your pet better if you compare his natural circumstances to the conditions he experiences in your home. Try to imagine the world from the perspective of your parrot.

At Home in the Jungle and in the Desert

Parrots are native to tropical and moderate zones in Central and South America, Asia, Africa, New Zealand, New Guinea, and Australia. Some species live in jungles; others, on forested mountain ranges; a few live in deserts or in areas with few trees. A very few species even live above the tree line and can tolerate freezing temperatures. The most colorful parrots are the lories, but not all parrots are brightly colored. Some have camouflage colors, and some are even black. In dense thickets, the Amazon's green coloration helps camouflage the bird. The smallest of all parrots is the Pygmy Parrot, which is about four inches (10 cm) long. The largest parrots, at about forty inches (1 m), are the Hyacinth Macaws.

An Introduction to Parrot Biology

The most characteristic feature of parrots is their powerful, curved bill. The striking form of the bill is an adaptation to the kind of life that parrots live. With the exception of the lories and a few other species that eat soft foods, parrots live primarily on seeds, nuts, and fruit. They are specialized in cracking hard shells and hulling seeds. The upper mandible is jointed at the skull and can move upwards. In parrots that eat fruits with hard shells, there are so-called "filing notches" in the lower edge of the bill that the bird uses to sharpen the cutting edges of the lower mandible. These notches also help the bird to hold food, and he uses them to file or rasp at hard shells that need to be weakened before they will crack. The lower mandible can slide back and forth slightly, which helps in hulling seeds. But the bill has other functions besides the preparation and consumption of food: It acts as a third foot in climbing, for example. The muscular tongue, which is equipped with taste buds, can also be used in grasping objects, in holding them, and in climbing, the latter being an especially important activity for some species. The bill is also used in the exchange of caresses. Parrots gently scratch each other and engage in mutual, social

Understanding Parrots

grooming. And in times of danger, the bill is a formidable weapon that is highly effective against certain enemies.

The feet and legs are adapted to the particular mode of life, too. In the parakeet genus *Cyanoramphus*, for example, they are designed for running and jumping. In the climbing birds, they aid in climbing. A typical climbing foot has two toes pointing forward and two backward. Like the bill, the toenails have several functions. Most large parrots hold their food in their toes and eat, so to speak, with their hands. Ability to fly is related to the native habitat. Species that have to forage over large territories and live in deserts or in areas with few trees are far more powerful fliers than the jungle dwellers. As a rule, species with long tail feathers fly very well, and species with short tail feathers are the better climbers.

Parrot Society

In the wild, parrots join together in large or small groups. Whatever they do, be it foraging, changing location, or sleeping, they do as a group. Some species even nest in colonies, but most parrots retire as pairs to breed. Even if parrots live in a large group, the pairs live monogamously, staying with their chosen partners for life. I used the word "chosen" deliberately here, for parrots will not accept just any member of the opposite sex as a marriage partner. This is one of the main reasons why it is so difficult to breed parrots in captivity. Because the flocks kept in captivity are relatively small, it can easily happen that these flocks will not contain any compatible couples.

Breeding Habits

Parrots usually breed in caves and hollows, selecting hollow trees, chinks in cliff walls, and sometimes empty termite hills as nesting sites. Some species lay their eggs on the bare floor; others make nests of small twigs or rotting wood. Smaller species usually breed twice a year; the larger ones, only once. Depending on species, there are two to eight eggs in a clutch. The eggs are round and white. Usually it is just the female that incubates the eggs, although both sexes of the cockatoos do. Both sexes, or sometimes primarily the male, are responsible for feeding the young. The young birds receive the somewhat softened and predigested food from their parents' crops. Feeding from the crop is a sign of affection between an adult male and female, too, and is part of the mating

Understanding Parrots

ritual. Parrots imprinted to human beings, lacking a partner of their own species, will often give this love offering from the crop to their human partner.

Body Language

Like human beings, animals are to some extent able to express their feelings and moods without the use of words. Your parrot, too, will express his pleasure or displeasure by means of the body language he would ordinarily use with others of his own kind. **Thin with Fear:** There are many loud sounds in our world, and it is clear that your parrot will be startled if a jet plane makes a sonic boom while breaking the sound barrier. If you look at your parrot at such a moment, you will see that he has become very thin. He has drawn all his feathers close to his body and stretched out his neck. When he has calmed down, his plumage will fluff out again, and he will look a little fatter. If you happen to live in an area where loud sounds like this occur often, the fear reaction may disappear. It may even happen that your bird will start to imitate these noises.

If he makes himself very thin during warm weather, spreading his wings and opening his bill at the same time, then he is simply too hot, and a shower might well be in order.

A parrot makes himself slim when he is afraid. The body is stretched out, and the feathers are drawn in close to the body.

Plump well-being: If your parrot sits on his perch looking like a fluffed up ball, possibly with one leg drawn up, and if he clicks softly with his bill at the same time, then he is utterly contented, and you should leave him in peace to enjoy his blessed state. His eyelids may flutter, and it will not be long before they close altogether while your bird takes a little nap.

If, however, he spends an unusually long amount of time sleeping every day, possibly with his bill tucked into his feathers, then he is either exhausted or sick.

Stretching: After your bird has finished his midday nap of about an hour, he will feel refreshed and ready to go again. Sometimes, after his siesta, he will stretch a wing and a leg

Understanding Parrots

on the same side. Or he may raise both wings, perhaps only once, perhaps several times. That means he is stretching as parrots like to stretch.

Mock attacks: After his nap, a parrot will soon be eager to play and romp a little. He will signal his playful intent to attack by raising the feathers on his head, the nape of his neck, and

This cockatoo is taking a nap. When parrots are sleeping very soundly, they often stick their heads into their feathers.

his back. He makes himself feel strong by creating the optical illusion of greater size. This raising of the feathers is clearly different from the cozy, fluffed up appearance of comfortable repose. The bird no longer looks like a soft, round ball. Now his feathers look rough and ruffled.

Aggression: If your parrot spreads his wings, opens his bill, and hacks into the air with it, then he is angry. Aggressive behavior of this kind can be meant as a warning, or it may immediately precede an actual attack. I was able to observe this kind of attack behavior when I once brought Vasco and my Amazon, Manaos, together. The two birds clearly did not care for each other. They went at each other like two fighting cocks, using not only their bills but also kicking each other in the belly (see photo, page 45). When I tried to separate them, I got my own share of slashes from their bills. The raised crest of a cockatoo betrays his excitement or aggression in an immediately obvious way. The South American Hawk-headed Parrot signals a threatening mood by raising the long feathers on the back of his head and neck into an imposing collar.

Parrots will beat their wings fiercely and emit a wild, jungle shriek either to intimidate a possible adversary or to demand attention.

Understanding Parrots

Inspiring fear, calling for attention: Sometimes a parrot will beat the air audibly with his wings and accompany this abrupt action with a wild scream. This sudden aggressive behavior is designed to inspire fear in a potential adversary, and I can testify that it is highly effective. Vasco will do this, too, if I have failed to respond to his persistent calls. Not only does he want to startle me, but he also wants to draw my attention.

Demands and requests: If we are in the room and Vasco wants something, he will usually whistle on one note and flutter his wings lightly, as if to suggest that he is too helpless to help himself. Then he will bite at one of his toenails the way a human might express impatience by biting his fingernails.

Embarrassment: A parrot can feel embarrassed, perhaps because he feels he is being watched too closely. He will react in somewhat the same way that a human being would. He will scratch his head, or shift his weight from one leg to the other. Often he will turn around 360 degrees or start to eat.

Expressions of affection: Do not force anything! That is the be-all and end-all of keeping a parrot. Let your bird do as he will, provided he is not being outright destructive. You can,

of course, pick him up if you feel the impulse; but it is better if you let him come to you of his own accord. Judging from my experience, I would say parrots tend to come seeking attention too often rather than too seldom.

If Vasco has not been with me for a while, either because he has been occupied elsewhere or has been sleeping, he will come waddling after me, marching across all the furniture in his path. Then he asks me to scratch his head. He comes toward me slightly stooped and nodding all the time. The gesture is perfectly clear: He wants his head scratched. All parrots want this because in the wild the birds do this for each other. One bird scratches another's head with his bill. We should not use a whole hand. One or two fingers are quite enough for such a small head. The whole hand would be too much and would frighten the bird.

If you scratch the way your bird likes it, you will be rewarded. Your parrot will nibble on your finger with his bill. You need not worry that he will bite you. He is "petting" you back. Unfortunately, many people misunderstand this overture of affection. Expecting to be bitten, they pull their fingers back. This rapid motion can frighten the bird, and then he may well actually bite, acting out of momentary fright, not ill will.

Understanding Parrots

Nibbling gently on a finger is one of a parrot's ways of expressing affection.

Although parrots love to be scratched on the head, they heartily dislike it if you try to scratch their backs or bellies (although there are some exceptions to this general statement). Scratch your parrot only where he likes to be scratched. He will even show you the exact spot by presenting the top, the side, or even the bottom of his head to your hand. Watch his eyes as you scratch him. The pupils of the eyes register your bird's pleasure, contracting and expanding in sheer delight.

Your parrot will be particularly grateful to you if, while you are scratching him, you release the feathers that are just coming in from their sheaths. You should not pull at these feathers unless they have grown out far enough; otherwise, you will hurt your bird. If he shrinks back,

you will know you have been too forceful. It is also pure torture for your bird if you pet him against the grain of the feathers.

If he has had enough scratching and stroking, he will move away from your hand or push your finger away with his bill.

Are Parrots Intelligent?

The question of intelligence in parrots is hotly debated. Where earlier behavioral scientists were somewhat excessive in their praise of parrot intelligence, they tend now to be more cautious. But this much we can say: Parrots show a remarkable ability to learn and imitate. They also "invent" games to keep themselves amused and tricks to attract human attention. Manaos will cry pathetically if he wants us to pay attention to him, and if Vasco gets no response

Almost all parrots like to have their heads scratched. Use just one finger, not your whole hand.

Understanding Parrots

Has anyone ever brushed your hair with a wire brush? That is how it feels to a parrot if you stroke him against his feathers.

with his calls, he will startle us into attentiveness. We fall for his tactics and take pity on the poor creature. He has gotten what he wanted. And there is no doubt in my mind that Vasco is consciously imitating me by raising his wings after I raise my arms.

Behavioral scientists say that it takes a high level of development for an animal to be able to imitate. But as far as I am concerned, we do not have to measure the parrots' intellectual capacities precisely in order to be able to enjoy the antics of these imps of the jungle.

Books for Further Information

All About Parrots
Arthur Freud: Howell Books

Encyclopedia of Lovebirds and Other Dwarf Parrots
Matthew M. Vriends: TFH Publications

Parrot Guide
Cyril H. Rogers: TFH Publications

Parrots of the World
TFH Publications

Starting an Aviary
Matthew M. Vriends: TFH Publications

This Is the Parrot
Carl Plath & Malcolm Davis: TFH Publications

Index

Index